To Jean & Jaz
my tw[o]

Foresight with Hindsight
and
More Memoirs

who have always encouraged my writing
Much love
Lesley xx

Published by Leaf Books Ltd 2010

Copyright © The Authors

www.leafbooks.co.uk
Leaf Books Ltd.
GTi Suite,
Valleys Innovation Centre,
Navigation Park,
Abercynon,
CF45 4SN

Printed by Jem
www.jem.co.uk

ISBN-13: 978-1-905599-60-8
Cover images © Cecilia Morreau

Contents

Introduction		5
Winner		
Piano Pieces	Diana Mitchener	9
Runner-up		
Foresight with Hindsight	Jane Common	13
Commended		
Marmalade	Jo Austen	17
I Thought It Was All Over	Trina Beckett	19
If I could only	Suzanne Bellenger	23
Lost	Pascale Bientot	27
Going Downhill	P. de Burlet	31
Girl Friday	Tracy Burton	35
Precious Years with Mother	Dolly Carter	39
Why? Because	Wendy Craig	41
Things Fall Apart	Jane Croft	45
Long Ago or Far Away	Ian Cundell	49
Euthanasia for Tortoises	Frank Ferrie	53
Threads	Lesley Fuller	55
Coat	Sue Gill	57
The Silence of the Children	David Grubb	61
Prospectors	Tamara Guhrs	65
Belong	Ursula Hurley	69
Stickers	Paul Jenkins	73

Jon-Paul	Freda Love Smith	75
The Cigarette Girl	Liz Martinez	77
The Point Of A Pendulum	Liz Martinez	79
Crows in the Toilet	Alison McNaught	81
Winning	Moira McPartlin	83
Legs Eleven, go to Heaven	Eithne Nightingale	85
Dad Looking Sideways	Amy O'Neil	89
My Dad	Clarissa Pattern	93
The Edge of El Dorado	Karen Phillips	95
Sometimes it's the Sound of the Telling	Clare Potter	99
Marianne, Me and the Giant Crustaceans	Brenda Ray	101
A Bomb in the Airing Cupboard	Joyce Reed	105
The Journey Home	Claire Riviere	107
Reds Under the Bed	Nick Robinson	111
Camping in France/ En Famille	Sylvia Sanderson	115
Strange Fruits	David Craig Smith	119
A Bright Enough Lad	Meic Stephens	123
Frozen in Time	Christine Tennent	129
The Time Traveller's Disappointment	Jennie Tripp	133
The Red Velvet Jacket	Jayne Walter	137
Do-Re-Mi-Oh-No	Lauren Williamson	141
Wednesday's Child	Georgina Wilson	145
Author Biographies		149

Introduction

Over the winter of 2009/2010, Leaf Books held its first ever Mini-Memoir competition. We invited our entrants to submit 'an extract from your own life in 1,000 words or fewer', and we suggested and duly received work on several topics including childhood, war, travel writing, family, school, work, community projects, political activism and allotments.

The competition was a resounding success: we received hundreds of entries from novice writers and established authors alike. A new competition is always a bit of a gamble as we never quite know what the uptake will be, but suffice to say we were quietly astonished at the number of entries we received to this one, and we spent a while pondering why it proved so popular. We guessed that the competition brief – the broad list of possible topics and the emphasis on writing from experience – made people who perhaps felt daunted by the notion of penning a piece of creative writing from scratch realise that they did indeed have a story to tell.

Indeed, one thing we became aware of this time around was that many of these authors, including some of the successful ones, were relatively new and sometimes even first-time writers. There was, on occasion, a slight, wholly understandable and frankly rather charming lack of polish to these more novice pieces that did not affect our judgement to the extent it might've done in a different sort of competition. Writing style is hugely important but content even more so, and that seemed truer still in the case of these very personal memoirs; the rawness of the writing, in many cases, was inherently touching. Certainly the sense that an author was feeling his or her way a little tentatively along the first few steps of the writing process did not really diminish the impact of many of these stories: in fact, knowing from the writing style that this was the first time an author had put pen to paper (or finger to keyboard) helped to convey the compulsion that author felt to tell this one important story.

One of the most impressive pieces from a novice writer is 'Precious Years with Mother' by Dolly Carter, a reminiscence of a childhood in India from an author now in her late seventies. This memoir, as her biography states, is her first attempt at writing, and to have inspired such an attempt is very gratifying for us as publishers. And it's an astonishingly accomplished piece of work from a beginner – it's written in the second person, which is no mean feat, the detail in the writing is hugely evocative ('The red you coughed up was assumed to be blood. My sister, a doctor in later years, told me that it was chilli dust...') and the sense of place is crystal clear – 'we would feast, eating off large banana leaves; masala fish wrapped in a fragrant coriander chutney' – one sense skilfully employed to trigger countless others.

The range of topics covered by the entries was extensive, and made for an interesting and varied judging experience. The more unusual experiences always leapt out at us ... from Jane Common's 'Foresight with Hindsight' (after which the competition anthology is named), detailing the narrator's surprisingly responsibility-filled stint as a telephonic tarot-card reader, to David Craig Smith's 'Strange Fruits' about the narrator's pharmacist-father's wondrous rainbow-coloured and everything-flavoured creations ('What other boy had a magician for a father who could charm him back to health with green raspberry tonic, red lemon linctus or blue banana syrup?'), to David Grubb's haunting, devastating, ultimately hopeful description of the Rwandan refugee camps in 'The Silence of the Children' ('Here is a boy in one of the classrooms who is telling the class about how he loved his parents, the animals they kept, the school he attended, the way the soldiers came, how the soldiers cut his hands off ... Then others tell their stories to prove they are still alive').

There was, of course, no one topic more likely to win the top prize than any other but we all thought it fitting, in the end, when a war story proved to be the overall winner: war stories, alongside school stories (also well represented in the anthology) made up the largest category and it pleased us to be able to reflect that in our choices. 'Piano Pieces' by Diana Mitchener was our favourite example of the genre: complete in itself and packed with evocative detail, emotionally deep and narratively uncomplicated, and stylistically very accomplished: Mitchener perfectly capturing the innocent, excited, poignantly hopeful voice of its youthful narrator that renders the story enormously touching without ever being sentimental. The metaphor of the narrator's father 'playing the war on the piano' is what holds the piece together – its internal cohesion is striking.

We could not even begin to fit all the pieces that impressed us into the anthology, but we feel that we've selected a high quality and representative collection of the topics we received. Our thanks to everyone who entered our first ever memoir competition ... and to those who were inspired to write for the very first time, we very much hope you continue.

Piano Pieces

by Diana Mitchener

Upstairs at 17 Britannia Road there is a bedroom for Mummy and Daddy, a bedroom for Anne (not Anne and Pat because Pat has gone to heaven), a bedroom for me and Isobel and a play room. But at night when the sirens go Daddy carries us downstairs to sleep on mattresses under the staircase. Then the bombs start falling. And what happens is that you hear a very thin whistle that gets louder and louder until you have to cover your ears and then there is a huge crash and the house shakes. If it shakes a lot the grown-ups say, 'That was very close,' and later Daddy goes out to see whose house has been hit. Sometimes he brings us shrapnel for our collection.

On very noisy nights Daddy plays Chopin's *Bump-de Bump* very loudly on the piano.

And what happens in the music is that everyone is woken up by bombs and cannons and they run to the walls of the town and see enemy soldiers attacking them. So all the men hurry to put on battle clothes over their pyjamas and the ladies help them to pull on heavy army boots. Then the men run out and fight. They keep fighting until the ladies say, 'Never mind. We'll make you a nice pot of tea.' When the ladies take the tea to the men and see the enemy throwing bombs at the walls they get very angry. They fetch everything they can and throw down chairs and books and chamber pots full of wee until in the end the enemy can't stand it anymore and gallop away and everyone jumps up and down and says, 'Hurrah! We've beaten you!'

And that is how Daddy plays the war on the piano.

One day I come home and there is a policeman at the door. I have to go next door to Mrs Dodds for tea. Isobel is already there, crying, her mouth pulled wide like a letter box. Mrs Dodds cuts bread with strawberry jam but Isobel won't eat. Daddy comes home in a taxi and runs in through the front door without waving to us.

That night I am put in bed with Daddy. He is crying into his pillow and I wake up and say, 'Why are you crying?' He says, 'Mummy's gone to Pat.' But I say, 'Perhaps she has just gone to Grandma Filkin's.'

I wait for her to come home and give us a hug like last time but she never does.

All over the house, people are crying; sobs from Anne, wails from Isobel, tears and sniffs from Daddy and long whispered 'Oh! Oh!'s from Grandma Apple who has come to look after us.

Now it is Daddy who shuts himself in the front room. He plays high, quiet melodies like Mummy singing with lower notes creeping sadly in and swelling up underneath.

That Sunday after we have been put to bed I hear the piano music begin in a deep blue sky. The Evening Star comes out smiling. Then other little stars peep out on high notes and sprinkle light across the purple. Big families like The Plough and Orion with the belt of three sisters say, 'We're here now,' and stand out boldly. It is like looking out of the bedroom window before the blackout closed out the stars, when you felt safely tucked up in bed and Mummy and Daddy told you fairy stories.

Then one of the stars slips. And another. I get up and listen at the top of the stairs. More stars slip and tumble and the rising chords are too weak to push them up again. I run downstairs to warn Daddy before Orion snaps and hangs broken in the sky. I open the door, which I am not supposed to do, and see Daddy at the piano letting the stars crash down in juddering chords. His face is rubbery with tears and his hands are fat and red.

'Daddy!' I run to him and he turns to feel for me and holds me close.

'Where's Mummy?' I ask him and he says:
'She's dead. Mummy's dead.'

The sirens start up with a low moan then a wail. German planes drone in the sky. Ack-ack guns go BANG! BANG! BANG! and waves of bombs whistle down.

We huddle tightly together under the stairs in our siren suits and sleeping bags: Anne, Isobel, Daddy, and the empty space which is Mummy.

1. CHOPIN's *'Bump-de-bump'*: *Polonnaise in A major Opus 40, No 1*
2. CHOPIN's *'Tristesse'*: *Etude in E major, Opus 10, no 3*

Foresight with Hindsight
by Jane Common

I can't recall now, nearly two decades on, which stop on the Underground I alighted at to get there but I do remember that the area had a gloomy end of the line feel to it, even though there is no end of the line on that particular stretch of tube – it's a circle.

In my memory, it was always raining – damp drizzle – as I crossed the busy road and then turned left at the corner shop down the dark alley and then left again to the wooden door to the shed that housed the place. I wished I was in my basement flat, smoking roll-up cigarettes and drinking weak tea with my friends. They treated me with a sort of awe as I left the flat every day to go there. I was like a soldier, off to the trenches, to return six months later with stories of the terrible but beautiful things I'd seen.

The interior of the shed was panelled with dark wood, heavy with cigarette smoke, redolent of a bookmakers in a hard-up part of town. We, the employees, sat at desks arranged in one large bank in the centre, cordoned off from each other by panels of plywood. I sat next to John, a wiry chain smoker. When neither of us was on the phone, John told me about his time in prison and, middle-class young lady that I was, I listened, excited.

My favourite part of the working day was when the city-trader rang John and, through the plywood, I'd hear him barking out instructions like gun-fire. 'Buy the sugar'; 'sell the tin'. It seemed incredible that some high-flying banker man in the city phoned our little shed for advice on his day's trading. But then we were, according to the adverts in the backs of magazines, the country's best tarot card readers – pay £1 a minute for the privilege of phoning us.

If I wasn't on the phone when John was talking to the trader

– and if we were on the phone for fewer than forty minutes an hour we were in trouble – I'd peer round the plywood to see if John had actually laid out the cards. He never had.

I always laid out the cards – I'm a stickler for instruction – as I'd been taught in my three-hour training session. I'd tell the person on the other end of the phone to stop me when some sort of vibration echoed, from my hand, down the phone line, to their subconscious. And then I'd ask them what they wanted to know about. Invariably they wanted to know about love.

That wasn't what our scruffy Glaswegian colleague with the clothes pegs in her hair wanted to talk about though.

'You're going to be hit by a bus, hen,' she shrieked down the phone one day at an unlucky caller. 'Dinnae leave the house tomorrow.'

'Yer man's hae-ing an affair,' she informed another.

She was warned not to tell the truth – the grim bits anyway. But she wouldn't cease her dire outpourings and, a few weeks after I'd started, she was sacked.

I don't know if I had the gift. I like to think I did, a little.

'A blonde-haired woman is making trouble in your life,' I told one woman.

'My husband has just left me for my best friend,' she gasped. 'She's blonde.'

Most people, I hoped, would put the phone down after a conversation with me, and feel, in some way, better about their lives. One woman – a posh sort of lady – who had recently been diagnosed with cancer would phone and ask to be put through to me. I'd go through the motions of reading her cards but really we both knew that all she wanted was to chat. About how terrified she was – about the long, dark nights she spent, fear seeping through her as insidiously as the cancer itself. She couldn't express that fear to any of her loved ones because it would frighten them. But to me, someone who existed only out there in the ether, she could say anything.

But there was one man I couldn't help and it was shortly after my conversation with him that I gave the job up.

'You're going through a bad time,' I told him. He was pretty mono-syllabic but he sounded miserable. 'I can see, from the cards, that in four weeks things are going to improve.'

'I won't be here in four weeks,' he said.

'Where will you be?' I said coolly, as if he might be off travelling around India, even though I knew what he meant. *Try to pretend it's not happening ....*

'I'll be dead,' he said and then the blood pumped fast and hot through my body as he detailed, exactly, what he was going to do.

'Suicide,' I scribbled on a bit of paper, which I waved at one of the supervisors. She rushed into the glass booth in the corner of the room where the manager sat, listening in to calls to see who was performing properly. I watched as he pushed some buttons to listen in to my call and pressed record. *All calls like this had to be recorded ....*

The supervisor handed a post-it note to me. 'Samaritans,' it read, and there was a phone number next to it.

'You should phone the Samaritans,' I said, as calmly as I could.

I don't think the man wrote the number down. There was just silence – as if, by mentioning the Samaritans, I'd let him down somehow, put him in a box and passed him on.

'The cards really do show me that your life is going to turn around,' I told him, panicking.

The line went dead. And even now, all these years later, I still wonder what happened to him – whether he did wait for a month until life improved.

Marmalade

by Jo Austen

My mother makes marmalade. It takes days. It is like magic. It is important, an annual event celebrated like birthdays or Christmas. She likes all the things you have to do; she likes it to be complicated, time-consuming.

She scrubs the kitchen first; everywhere has to be spotless. Jam jars are put in the oven to sterilise and then reappear later as inedible cookies, steaming slightly, on a tray. The pressure cookers come next; large steel pans that smell of hospitals, not cooking, or perhaps the faint scent of over-cooked Brussels sprouts or beans.

Oranges arrive and take their positions on the formica worktops; brushing against the bags of green netting. It takes lots of oranges; and lots of sugar. One year there was a sugar shortage. My mother went exploring on her push bike, finding shops that would sell her a bag of sugar. It must have been like this in the war, with rationing; scrimping, saving, not enough preserves.

You cannot eat the oranges just as they are. I tried once: it was like sucking a lemon and my mouth curled in on itself.

When the oranges are boiling the smell gets everywhere. It should smell of Spain (where the oranges grow) or Scotland (where marmalade is officially made) or Victorian kitchens, a reminder of the days when you made your own food; brought your shopping home wrapped in brown paper bags, and had pink hands from kneading bread. What it does smell of is a sweet factory, the sugar sitting heavy in the air.

My mother's favourite part is when she drops a little of the amber mixture on to a plate to see if it will set. She is happy; she is creating, making spells. She strokes the thermometer lovingly, keeps the ladle shiny; wears her smile like her apron, tied up at the back. When it is right, she spoons it into the jars, seals them quick, a circle of parchment, then a plastic one, then a rubber band. The bands are multicoloured rings taken from giant hands.

One year, she let me write the labels. We bought some fancy ones with orange borders especially. I wrote 'Marmalade - 1979' on each one. But it was not the same, not for her; she wrote them herself again in the next year.

The marmalade goes in the cupboard. Not many people eat it; the jam gets stored, building up vintages, a diary of marigold events, slowly turning brown. It does not matter to her that they do not get eaten.

My father likes to pick blackberries, foraged, salvaged, pilfered from the English waysides. He likes blackberry crumble and blackberries and custard; but most of all he likes blackberry jam. My mother does make it for him sometimes too, but then it is just a job.

I Thought It Was All Over
by Trina Beckett

Bright lights spun round my bedroom. Tyres crunched on gravel. A metallic door clanged shut. Urgent, muted voices. Footsteps on the stairs. Heavy, unnatural breathing close to my door. I clutched my pink teddy so tightly one of his button eyes popped out on its pin. A disinfectanty smell permeated the air as Father came into my bedroom.

'Mother has to go away. Stay in your room.' He closed my door.

'Mind the wallpaper.' Mother's voice, hoarse and crackly. Something scraped along the landing wall. My baby sister was crying. I pulled on my dressing gown and started out of my room. Father blocked my way. Rubbing away frost patterns on icy windows, I watched the dancing rear lights of a large van as it bounced down the rough track away from our house.

'Baby needs feeding.' Father's eyes were wet. In 1956 men didn't cry, the phrase 'New Man' unheard of.

'I'll see to her.' I plucked my baby sister from her cot, soothing her as I went downstairs. 'Take her for a minute.' Father held her awkwardly. 'Not like that; she can't hold her head up on her own yet.'

'Mother's obviously taught you a thing or two.'

'I just watch.' The feed ready, my father handed back the whimpering bundle. I cuddled her close. She gulped down every drop. 'Pass me a clean nappy.' Father hesitated. 'In the boiler cupboard: from the pile on the left, so the same ones don't get used all the time.' I felt older than my five years.

'You won't be going to school tomorrow.'

'Can't Auntie pop in to give you a hand?'

'No. No-one can.'

'I can walk to school and back on my own. I'll make baby's

feeds, so you'll have enough when I'm not here.' Father smiled, but looked unhappy at the same time. He paused, nibbling at a torn fingernail.

'Mother has diphtheria.' The word bolted through my heart like forked lightening. There was a full stop after diphtheria, marking the end of a life. 'We have to stay in the house.' The truth behind his words sunk in. My mouth felt dry.

'Baby's been crying more than usual.'

'She was cross, that's all, but we need to keep an eye on her, and you must say straight away if your throat feels sore. Come here.' He held me tight. I wasn't use to such close contact; stale pipe smoke filled my nostrils. 'They'll be back early to fumigate the house.' Baby fed and changed, I dragged my blankets into her room, cocooning myself against the plummeting temperatures of the midwinter night.

After what seemed like an eternity, half-waking, half-sleeping, I heard my father's voice.

'They're here. Stay with baby.' I stared through frosty panes as bulky figures pulled a long tube from a van. One looked towards the house, two dark holes instead of eyes, and another for a mouth. I prayed my father wouldn't let them in. Rustling sounds floated upstairs.

'I've got to put this up all the chimneys, to stop fumes escaping.' Father peered round the door, clutching a wad of crinkly paper. He was covered in soot. 'Wrap yourselves up and go into the verandah.' Stepping into the flimsy lean-to, cold shot through my body.

'George! George!' He wasn't moving: eyes and mouth wide open. Why wasn't he in the kitchen? Mother always put him in the kitchen at night. I followed the sounds of voices, crackly, like failing radio signals.

'It's George. I think he's dead.' I was trying hard not to cry. There was an expression on my father's face I hadn't seen before. He was no longer my place of safety.

'I can't worry about a goldfish at a time like this.' Yellow vapour was seeping down the stairs, shrouding the creatures I'd seen earlier.

'Baby needs feeding,' I mouthed.

'Later. Go back.' His face softened. 'They won't take long.' An hour later, the house was quiet, the final yellowy fumes wisping from the outside lavatory. 'They're off now. You can wave if you like.'

'At the monsters?'

'I don't know any monsters called Fred and Bob, do you?' The glimmer of a smile.

'Is Mother ...?' The glimmer vanished. He rubbed his ear, and looked away. 'Someone will leave a note later.' We didn't have a phone.

For the next four days, I watched, as aunts and neighbours deposited stews, cakes and shopping halfway down the garden path, before scurrying away. School work was delivered, with strict instructions not to be returned. I adopted the mantle of parent, my normally rocklike father sinking into helpless despair.

'You're a good girl' was the best he could manage. Each afternoon he trudged down the path to pick up a large brown envelope. All he ever said to my enquiring glance was 'No change.' The fifth evening, he rushed up the path like an excited child. 'She hasn't got diphtheria! It's a streptococcal throat.' His eyes glistened. A 'septic cockle' throat sounded horrific, but it was what Mother *didn't* have that mattered. My world turned itself the right way up again. I was fizzy with happiness.

Next day at the school gates, my father gave me a self-conscious goodbye kiss, and was gone. I rushed up to my best, best friend, ready to enthral her with tales of monsters and yellow fumes. She drew back.

'I sit by Susan now.' I edged closer; she retreated. 'Mummy says to keep away from you.' She bit her lip.

'It was only a septic cockle throat. You can come to tea next week if you like,' I pleaded. Susan sidled up, stopping, as if barred by an invisible barrier. She linked arms with my best, best friend. As one, they skipped away. I had emerged from my dark tunnel, enjoyed a fleeting time in the sunshine, only to fall straight down a black hole, my childhood contaminated beyond healing. I have never allowed myself another best, best friend.

If I could only

by Suzanne Bellenger

I have to choose my mother's clothes. They said bring underwear, but it seems too personal to ask what. Do they just mean pants, or should she be dressed like an elaborate doll, perfect in every unseen detail? Somehow the underwear seems the most intrusive, the side that never showed and I worry about getting it wrong. I open her underwear drawer to pants neatly layered, small hillocks of bras and spongy balls of tights and stockings. Stockings? Would she want to wear stockings and suspenders? It suggests an intimacy she would not wish to share with a stranger. I can accept that someone else will dress her, but would she want them pulling up her stockings and attaching them to the fiddly clasps? And would they clip them at the back for her, or leave them undone, easier than groping around her lifeless legs?

I leave these for the moment and consider the rest of her underwear. The old and perfunctory I dismiss automatically, but that still leaves too many choices. Whether to go for black, white or a daring colour? Should it be pretty, sexy even or something plain that won't tell stories? What would my mother want, she who carefully hid her personal life and even her dying from me? I can't choose these without getting lost in her and I stop and sit on the bed, indulging.

It was years ago and she was helping me tidy my room – again. Every drawer had been pulled out and emptied as we worked through the mounds. I was distracted by each uncovered memory, carefully stored but then ignored. I peeled cards from their envelopes, read old letters, and was instantly immersed in forgotten tales. 'Let's just get it done, you can read those later,' she told me and reluctantly I had put my treasures aside, saving them up as my reward for finishing. She would be telling me off now, sitting on her bed when there was work to be done.

I try it another way, think about dressing myself. Oh – of course, how can I choose her underwear till I know what she's wearing? I open her wardrobe and am flooded by her scent. It's the sweetest smell I know and for a moment, she's there beside me. She has to be. How can her scent be present without her? At least it lets me pretend and I inhale slowly, trying not to gulp it down and use her up.

Suits, dresses, skirts, blouses, all carefully arranged by type and colour. What would she want as her final outfit? It's something we never discussed. I thought we'd gone through all the 'If you could only' games, where life's categories were distilled to a single selection. A favourite food or book, maybe a place or person, but we'd never chosen clothes. 'If you could only wear one thing again, Mother, what would it be?'

I'm blinded by her clothes and I have to shut the doors, keeping in her precious smell, and sit on the bed again. Should I buy her something new – this is a special occasion after all – but what if it didn't fit? Or didn't suit her? I am sure they wouldn't tell me, and it would be humiliating for her to be tugged and pushed into strange garments. Best to keep it something old, clothes she knows and will slip into like an old friend. At least she won't be alone.

In the end, I select a navy suit and cream, silk blouse. Despite the years dressed for hauling hay and stubborn sheep, she loved wearing tailored clothes. Sharp cuts and darts curved around her slight body and gave her an understated grace. Nothing floppy or floaty: she liked strong, guard clothes that warned you not to underestimate. I add some navy court shoes, heeled but not too high. Though why not? I needn't worry whether she can walk in them. Finally, jewellery. She'd always wear a large brooch pinned to her lapel, as if a diversion from herself. Should I hide her away with a favourite, or hold it back to keep her with me? I take a selection and decide to leave this to chance. I will pull one out at the undertakers and if my stomach flips and tells me 'No', I'll put my hand back in my pocket and slip out another.

I go back to the underwear. It is easier now I know her clothes, and it is as if she is guiding me. 'Nothing old or sensible please, but nothing that might be mocked.' So I go for white, lacy but not too pretty, something she might wear to visit the doctor. I want to give her stockings, tights seem so prosaic, but I have convinced myself that they will not attach the stockings properly. I remove the cellophane from an unopened packet of tights and carefully push my hand inside, nails curved into my palm. Even though they are new, I must check there are no holes. I'm still suspicious of the undertaker's concern and my mother would be appalled to go out wearing laddered tights.

I scrabble under the bed for an overnight bag – if only. I try to pack it as she would but the omissions won't let me be fooled. No books, no toiletries and most significantly, no change of clothes. Tomorrow, I will take it to the undertakers, the last people who will see my mother.

I just hope that they will dress her with all the care of a wedding, before sealing her from my love.

Lost

by Pascale Bientot

The night before my geography exam I come home and my sister's run away. She's left a note and taken the housekeeping. My mam's away and I'm supposed to be in charge. The note says 'London'.

I go round to my nan's. She's washing up after the boarders' tea. Cara's gone, I say, run away. I hand her the note. My nan dries her hands on the tea towel, turns the wireless off and fishes in her cardy pocket for her glasses. We sit down at the table and she reads the note.

My nan phones the police and reports a missing person, a child, she says, fifteen. The police come. They rummage about in Cara's room. I tell them the names of some friends she had at school, and no, there wasn't a boyfriend, not as far as I know. No, I don't think she knows anybody in London, she's never even been there. And no, I don't know why she's gone. They take the note away, and last year's school photograph, and the pillowcase for the sniffer dog.

We wait for phone calls, but none come. My nan rings round various rellos; nobody knows anything, but they're all ears. My mother has never had much sympathy in our family and you can imagine people smirking their faces off over our little tragedy.

The next day I go to school, but my mind's a blank. I tell Myra and she says to go home with her, but in the end I go back to my nan's. Nothing, she says, when I walk in, no news is good news. Yeah, I say.

She makes mince and dumplings and I eat it with Mr Fanshaw from the Electric Board. He says he's stumped; it's beyond him what kids think they're on about these days. Mr Fanshaw sneaks me one of his Number 6 when Nan's not looking, and I save it in my school bag for later. The police come – it's a woman this time

– and say nothing as yet, but no stone will be left unturned.

Then she wants to speak to me, alone. We go through to the front room, which is only used on séance days and at Christmas. Granda's mantelpiece clock from the miners' gala has a very loud tick. There's a smell of old soot from the chimney and a peppery scent of geraniums. The police woman – she says just call me Mandy – sits on the sofa and flicks through her paperwork. You've no idea what's behind this, she asks. I say I don't know. Was your sister … was Cara … was she happy at home, she says, I mean, she must've had a reason, if it's not a boyfriend thing. I shrug. She looks me crisply in the eye and in a different voice she says, Alice, it's vitally important that you tell us everything you know. They've been to Cara's school – where she used to go that is, she left there more than a year ago now. I shrug again.

My nan says what did the policewoman want then. Mandy, I say, she's called Mandy. Well what did Mandy want then, my nan asks. She says Mandy as though it's a disease. She's sticking golden ric rac braid onto the red felt jacket of a tiny beefeater doll. Her fingers aren't what they used to be and she's having trouble getting the braid in place. There's a small pile of dolls already finished and another pile of little red hats ready to go on. Shall I do the hats, I ask. But she doesn't answer. I didn't think she would. Plus she's forgotten I had an exam today.

Mandy says if I think of anything I'm to phone. I don't have to rack my brains very hard to know why my sister's gone. I consider telling my nan, but what's the point? It's not going to get Cara back, and anyway she's probably better off where she is.

Myra says it's daft to go to London; she says I'll never find Cara in a zillion years. Then the day before my mam's due back my sister rings up from a phone box. She thinks the whole thing's hilarious. She's found a job with some dodgy film thing, and is staying with a man, in Ladbroke Grove, just for now. Who's the man, I ask. It turns out he's forty-seven; don't say nothing, she says. This is for your ears only.

Then: why don't you come, she says, I'll give you the address if you promise to come. I have to get away before my mam's back or there'll be ructions. I walk to Gosforth High Street and stick my thumb out. Getting a lift is a piece of piss. Seven hours later a fat lorry driver from Aberdeen who kept on rubbing his crotch and smelt of BO drops me off at Finsbury Park and says get the tube from here lassie.

There's a map on the wall and a skinny girl with dyed black straggly hair is standing beside it. She fishes a half smoked cigarette out of her pocket and says have you got a light. I give her my matches. She lights the stub then ambles off keeping the matches. I watch her walk away. She's got no shoes on and her feet are filthy.

I find Ladbroke Grove on the map: I'll have to get the blue line then change onto the pink one. The blue line is the Piccadilly, so I follow the signs, through the tunnel and down the escalators, with everyone rushing past.

The summer of 1969 and my mother comes home to find the house empty. Alice and Cara, in a Ladbroke Grove bedsit, with a dodgy gas fire and a broken window, are getting drunk on cheap sherry and laughing and saying in silly voices, 'she can put that in her pipe and smoke it'.

Going Downhill

by P. de Burlet

When I was young, very young, I believed I was old. As old as time. It was perfectly logical. There had been no time before me. I had always existed.

I discovered I was wrong because I was about to celebrate a birthday.

'What is a birthday?'

'It's the anniversary of the day you were born.'

'What's an anniversary?'

I could see my mother was considering how to explain 'birthday'.

'It's a measure of time. Usually in years. You have been alive for four years.'

I could count to four but four what? Four times three hundred and sixty-five meant nothing. I was struggling.

'I have been alive for four years?'

'Yes.'

'How long have you been alive?'

'Forty-four years.'

'Is that a lot more than me?'

'Well, yes ... and then again ... no.'

'How long has Barbara been alive?'

'Barbara is eight years old so she has been alive twice as long as you.'

'If she is twice as old as me why is she unkind?'

My mother couldn't agree my sister was mean so she tried the distraction trick.

'What shall we have for tea?'

Right behind her, on the draining board, I could see a cascade of glossy pea pods so I said 'peas'.

But I still had questions as 'age' had become a mystery to be unravelled.

'And how old is Dad?'

'Your father is thirty-five.'

I didn't have to ask if thirty-five was less or more than forty-four. I knew he was younger than my mother even though he was the important one who wore a smart uniform and went off to work in the mornings. I liked his hat best as it had gold wings and a crown above the brim. I liked to feel the rough bumpiness of the wings but Dad was very anxious about sticky fingers.

I knew he was younger than my mother because at weekends, when the uniform was off, Dad was different. If the weather was good we went to the beach. At the beach everything came off and we didn't have to wear swimming costumes. Barbara usually put hers on but Dad didn't and I didn't. Mum didn't wear hers either but, with our help, she always scooped a large, shallow hole in the sand and then put up a big umbrella. Into the hole went my mother with all the supplies for the day and the umbrella neatly covered everything. When we called her or needed something, a towel or a sandwich or something, she would stick her head out. She was a turtle with a flowery nylon shell.

Me, Dad and Barbara would collect things on the beach, swim and play in the sand dunes. Sometimes we just lay on the warm sand and looked at the sea.

When we walked along the beach I could tell that other people liked the look of Dad. He had one leg that was thinner than the other and a slight limp. He said it was from something called 'polio' that he had as a boy. And one of his arms was badly scarred. Mum told me it was from an aeroplane crash. Anyhow, apart from the skinny leg and the funny arm, Dad looked perfect.

One day at the beach we were doing my favourite thing. We three climbed to the top of a big sand dune and, with Barbara and I each holding one of Dad's hands, we leaped and bounded down the hill. It felt like flying and we laughed and squealed all the way down and then begged to do it again. We trudged breathlessly to the top, turned and readied ourselves for the downhill.

I could see a woman at the bottom of the hill watching us. She stood still, partly in shade and partly in sun, and her skin was dappled black and gold. She didn't have a swimming costume on either. I was dazzled by this leopard woman with her black and gold breasts. Had Dad seen her too? I was about to point her out when Barbara gave me a slap.

'It's rude to stare.'

'Ready?'

'Ready.'

Dad held our hands tightly and off we went. I was swinging on Dad's arm and I felt like my bare feet hardly touched the ground. They did though and halfway down the hill one of my feet landed firmly on the sand and the broken bottle buried just under the surface. Dad felt my leg give way so he stopped and swung me up. We looked at the blood and the gaping flesh of my foot and I could feel his panic. Taking the broken bottle with us we carried on down the sand dune. The dappled woman at the bottom stretched out her hand to us. I think she said, 'Can I help?'

I could feel Dad hesitate so I yelled.

'No! I want Mum.'

Carrying me and pulling Barbara along he ran, calling for Mum.

She didn't panic. She wrapped my foot in a towel, handed out clothes and shoes and led us to the car. We left the umbrella behind.

That's how I knew that Dad was younger than Mum because he panicked and she didn't. She was a turtle after all.

Later, behind a door that said 'Minor Injuries', while my foot was stitched, I buried my face in Dad's shoulder where I could smell salt, sunshine and sweat.

A while after that, when I understood age a bit better but still not much about pain, Dad left us. He was too young to understand how much we loved him.

Girl Friday

by Tracy Burton

It was the day before payday, the last week of the summer holidays. Our mothers' purses were empty, we were bored and the only known cure for boredom was den-making.

Two hours ago, we'd crossed the bridge to the wasteland where we'd spent most of the balmy summer days. Now, with the promise of an afternoon's den-making, our spirits were high as we pushed through the waist-high scrub.

In front of me, Mucko grumbled about the film he'd wanted to see. There was a boil on his neck, red and angry; his mother would probably lance it later.

Peter was older than the rest of us and his word was God. No-one questioned his status, not even Beverley, who had what my mother called 'big bones' and used words I'd never heard of. Beverley thought Peter was wonderful; we all did.

That afternoon, he sprinted ahead, pushing aside brambles and stingy nettles. There was no-one as brave and fearless, I thought, as he disappeared.

Next to me, Debbie was fussing about gnats and behind us, red-faced and puffing, Beverley stuffed plush nuggets into her mouth. A brightly-coloured insect crash-landed on Debbie's arm, causing her to scream hysterically.

'It won't hurt you; it's a dragon-fly,' I said as it flew off. She shrugged, the stretchy halter-neck top she'd talked me out of buying last week showing off her figure to perfection.

Peter was striding back. 'Get a move on. I've found a great place for the den.'

Mucko and the two Chrissies raced ahead and I broke into a skip. Debbie had always detested these expeditions, but recently she seemed resigned to tagging along in her girly clothes.

I hated her sometimes. Often. But she was my best friend so I had to put up with her. 'There won't be any spiders, will there?' she whimpered. 'I hate spiders.'

'Don't be a sissy.' I tried not to shudder. I especially hated the big hairy ones, like the one blocking Peter's path now. He charged through its web, leaving it swinging desperately from a thread.

Peter was brilliant at finding dens. This time, it was a small brick building. There was no roof but most of the walls were standing. In one corner was a pile of wood that we could use for a table and chairs. It was going to be the best den ever.

'You girls clean the place up,' Peter said. I was about to spring into action, but he pointed at the bushes. 'Come on, I need help getting that over here.'

I wasn't sure who he was talking to, but Beverley was eating as though her life depended on it and Debbie wrinkled her nose daintily so I headed after him.

When we were out of earshot, he said, 'We'll be a family, stranded on a desert island.'

'Like Robinson Crusoe?'

'No, stupid. Swiss Family Robinson.' He was looking over his shoulder. 'We've been here years; the food's running out. I'll be father, decide what to do.'

And I'd be Friday, I thought. No, no. I'd be Mrs Robinson – Peter's strong, loyal wife. Mrs Robinson wouldn't be scared of spiders – or dragon-flies. This was good news as it ruled out Debbie – and Beverley's first love would always be food.

'Grab the end,' Peter yelled as we got close to an abandoned settee. I froze. Slugs, insects and spiders were crawling everywhere. 'Get a move on.' He rolled up his sleeves. 'Okay?'

I nodded and, teeth clenched, swept a hand across the damp cushions, clearing them of all forms of wildlife. A large, spindly-legged spider ran close by before changing direction. I breathed again.

We shoved and pushed the settee back to the hut. When we

got there, I pushed my hair out of my eyes and was greeted with a vision of loveliness: Debbie in white shorts and halter-neck.

I glanced down. My cheese-cloth top was scagged and grubby; worse, my new white daps – the daps I'd never put on before today – were covered in grass stains.

I wondered if I might survive the night if I explained to my mother how important it was to build a proper home on a desert island.

I tried to cheer up; I'd done okay for a girl. Mucko even gave me a thumbs up as I heaved the settee into its final position. I was mortified to see he was still watching me now. I stuck my nose in the air and turned just in time to see Peter handing his shirt to Debbie.

She was giving him the same angelic smile that always worked when she hadn't done her homework and Peter had that same stupid look on his face as our maths teacher.

Debbie, who'd been dressing herself since she was two, was suddenly having problems with an armhole. Peter seemed happy to show her what went where.

I wanted to look away but couldn't. The world might have ended, but for the sound of Beverley chomping behind me.

Chrissie and Chrissie were too busy trying to persuade her to part with two plush nuggets to notice, but Mucko was watching; which made it worse somehow. Then he started to fiddle with the buttons on his own shirt.

'It's not cold,' I hissed at him, praying no-one else had noticed. He was still undoing his buttons. 'I'm not cold. Mucko, stop it!'

Then Debbie let out a piercing scream. 'There's a spider on my arm! Get it off! Get it off me!'

And that was the moment my dream died. I watched, mesmerised, as Peter gently removed the offending creature from her arm, tossed it to the ground and stamped on it. Then Debbie's mouth, still open in alarm, disappeared under Peter's

37

lips for what seemed an eternity.

Mucko touched my arm. 'Poor little spider. Didn't stand a chance.'

I blinked rapidly to stop the tears spilling onto my cheeks.

'I'm going home,' I told him. 'Tell them I need to change my daps.'

Precious Years with Mother
by Dolly Carter

You were strong; you remained so after Dad left. You gave birth to five children but Dollet did not survive and died before I was born. I don't ever recall Papa living with us; I was very young when he went. Actually, you kicked him out and he fled back to Mumbai to his sisters; those women, aunts of mine, who had made your life so difficult. Papa was weak and didn't stand up for you. You were tough and stood up for all of us.

Our young lives were spent in the Parsee Colony in Pune and they were happy days. You worked hard, cooking by day for wealthy Parsees and at night, while we slept, you toiled away in your own little factory, grinding chillies and selling their caustic powder. Occasionally, you were able to afford to employ others to do this work but, more often than not, you worked alone.

On holy days, you would prepare food to sell and we would wait expectantly for you to return with an assortment of tasty leftovers and then we would feast, eating off large banana leaves; masala fish wrapped in a fragrant coriander chutney. Each tasty morsel popped into grateful little mouths.

You made sure that birthdays were special. I loved cheese and somehow you always produced a tin of the yellow delicacy for my delectation. I would carry it around throughout the day until temptation finally overcame me. It would be shared around by us and you would accept only the smallest fragment, popping it into your mouth with a tiny smile. I love cheese – all cheese – to this day but none tastes as fine as that precious little tin of processed, waxy stuff that you hunted down for me. We had little money to spare but it just never mattered. Somehow, you always found the energy to smile and you were such fun to be with.

The best days for our family were those when my older

brother, Jamshed, returned home for one month a year from his school, a place situated a day and a night's train ride away and run to benefit boys from poor homes. We would feast and make merry, Jamshed full of funny tales and mischief. You would tell him off and laugh at the same time, excusing his high spirits and rascal ways. How difficult it must have been for you to be parted from him for the other eleven months. You knew that there was no other way if he were to have any sort of an education. We girls fared better as the Parsee school for girls was right there in our town.

I was nine years of age when you became ill. You had coughed all my life; I would fall asleep to the familiar sound of it. The red you coughed up was assumed to be blood. My sister, a doctor in later years, told me that it was chilli dust. That highly prized pungent flavouring that you patiently ground, night after night, had been corroding the tissues of your lungs and slowly destroying your health. You died soon after. Your little terrier stopped eating and quietly pined away; no consolation in life for her.

Mum, we did what you would have expected us to do; we studied and worked hard. We missed you but we loved life and took that quality from you. I grew up strong and resilient; my childhood remained happy, despite the dreadful sorrow your death inflicted. Our friends and community cared for us. I had nine years with you and they were invaluable to who I was and who I became. Thank you, Mum.

Why? Because

by Wendy Craig

'*Yiati, Oondi? Yiati?* Why, Wendy? Why are you in Kritsa?'

My landlady's question is the one I have been dreading. Why am I here? I'm not exactly sure myself.

How can I explain in my stumbling Greek, to someone who does not speak a word of English, the deep love I feel for this country I first visited twenty-five years ago and have carried in my heart ever since? How can I tell her I left my apartment in New Zealand's largest city and came to this village in Crete on a whim? A wake-up-one-morning-and-decide-to-live-in-Greece-for-a-while whim. How can I make her understand that I came here by chance and felt intuitively that this was the right place for me?

It is difficult enough to express these feelings in English. But in Greek? For me, impossible. My phrase book doesn't go much beyond 'Where is the post office?' and 'I need a doctor.' It is no help at all for words of the heart.

I know that despite the complications of the long, long words, the myriad of word endings, the contrariness of irregular verbs, the confusion of letters that look like English ones but don't sound like them, and the capricious spellings, there are some parts of the Greek language that are very simple. Like 'why' and 'because'. One word for both. *Yiati*.

My landlady is becoming impatient. '*Yiati*, why?' she demands.

'*Yiati*, because,' I say.

'*Yiati, yiati*, because why?'

'*Mono yiati*, just because.'

'*Alla yiati yiati*, but why because?'

'*Yiati*,' I say and the words burst from me. 'Because I love it.'

We are sitting out on my tiny balcony, drinking spring water, eating pomegranates. It is nearly bedtime. In the soft grey of the night I can see her eyes gleaming.

'Listen,' I say. 'I want that I tell you a story.' In my heavily accented Greek, confident with vocabulary, shaky in grammatical knowledge, ignorant of any tense except the present, I begin.

'Before four years I am here in Crete with my daughter. We are staying in a hotel in Aghios Nikolaos for three weeks. One day my daughter is throwing bread to the fish in the lake and she throws herself in also.'

I am warming to my story now. Miming it. Adding dramatic gestures. Rising from my seat to show how my daughter emerged from the lake like Aphrodite from the deep, dripping not foam but streamers of lake weed.

With a magician's flourish I pretend to whisk away a tablecloth. 'The waiter from the taverna is taking the cloth and putting it round my daughter. My daughter is crying. She is green with ... (and I scramble for my dictionary) ... weeds.'

My landlady is shaking with laughter in the moonlight. 'Go on, go on,' she urges.

'One day I am coming to Kritsa. For many hours I walk around this village. I look. I think. The people and the houses please me. Then I am walking through the mountains. I am singing with happiness, much happiness, very much. Truly. I think that I am returning here sometime and I want that I live here.'

I fall silent then, lost in the memory of that day. It was early spring. Walking in the mountains above the village it seemed as if I was the only person in the entire world. An eagle soared high in the blue, blue sky above the peaks. The air was vibrating with the humming of bees and jingling bells of goats feeding in the thorn bushes. I felt, in those few hours, overwhelming joy.

'*Endaxi, endaxi*, okay, okay.' My landlady breaks the mood. Too practical for romantic reminiscence, she wants me to continue. 'And this time?' she asks.

'This time,' I continue, 'I am arriving in Crete at six in the morning.'

'Ha!' she interrupts. 'You don't like early mornings.'

'I know, but the aeroplane is cheaper in the night,' I tell her. 'I go to the bus at the airport and I say to the driver that I want that I go to the bus station for Aghios Nikolaos. We drive to Heraklion and we are driving and we are driving – to the bus station for Chania! I am not wanting that I go to Chania. I tell the inspector that this is not the bus station for me. He takes my bags and we go to another bus. He tells all the passengers what is happening to me.'

I am in full flight now, no longer embarrassed by my linguistic mistakes. My dictionary lies abandoned on the table. I act out the role of the inspector, complete with gruff voice and sweeping gesticulations. My landlady is on the edge of her seat, egging me on.

'I am shy. Everybody is saying, "*Po, po, po*," and smiling. We are driving and driving. Now I am thinking this is the road for me to the right bus station. So I stand up. Everybody says, "Sit down". We are driving more. Everybody says, "Stand up". The bus stops. Everybody says, "Get off". The bus goes. Everybody is waving.'

I pause for breath. My landlady wipes away tears of laughter.

'An old man gets off also and he carries my bags to the bus station. I buy a ticket for Aghios Nikolaos. In twenty minutes the bus is leaving so I sit under a tree. The bus starts. It is too early. I am shouting, "Stop! Stop!" and I am running that I get the bus. Then I am going to Aghios Nikolaos and then I am going to Kritsa. Here I see the "Room to Rent" sign and the garden and you and now I am living here.'

'*Nai*, yes,' she says. '*Oondi einai stin Kritsa*, Wendy is in Kritsa.' She stands up, slaps me on the back in farewell and goes up the garden path to her house, chuckling to herself in the starlight and muttering, '*Oondi stin Kritsa, Oondi stin Kritsa.*'

Things Fall Apart

by Jane Croft

'I'm afraid that half the textbooks still haven't arrived,' the Headmaster announced at the opening staff meeting of the academic year. 'Someone will have to go back to Freetown and get them.'

An eloquent silence followed in which no-one met his eye. It was a round trip of four hundred miles. Of those, the first and last seventy were comprised of dirt road and, worst of all, the rainy season wasn't over. No-one in their right mind would volunteer for the job. In the end we drew lots. That's why I found myself heading back to the coast I'd left only a fortnight earlier for that first trip up country when anxiety had been allayed by excitement and novelty. After seven hours on a wooden bench in the back of a lorry it has to be said that the novelty part had soon worn off. On the other hand, discomfort had been tempered by the thought that there would be no need to do this journey again until December. By then we'd be well into the dry season and the roads would be better. How wrong can a person be?

Despite all reservations, the first part of the trip went without a hitch. I reached Freetown and collected the books from the supplier. The following day I headed north again. The government bus took me as far as Makeni which marked the end of the metalled road. From there the journey had to be completed by local truck and these left from the lorry park at the edge of town. Getting a ride was not a problem: all the drivers' touts could spot a potential client a mile away through dense jungle on a moonless night. In a very short time I and my boxes were ensconced for the last leg of the expedition.

The road to Kabala was challenging at any time; after five months of rain it was truly hazardous. Water eroded deep gullies. Passing traffic churned the surface to red mud. Termites undermined the wooden planks that spanned the intersecting streams. At this season these were swollen torrents that poured off the hillsides. The air was sultry, thick as cotton wool with humidity from the frequent downpours. Everywhere huge puddles steamed in the heat.

The poda-poda crawled along the red road between towering walls of elephant grass. It was aptly named. An elephant standing two feet away would have been invisible amid that lush green growth. However, the lively West African pop music blaring from the radio rendered any encounters with wildlife unlikely. The truck itself resembled some rare and brilliant tropical insect, its bodywork vivid in magenta and purple and yellow. No less exotic, windscreen and dashboard were lavishly adorned with plastic flowers, furry dice, lucky charms, juju amulets, wooden carvings and, hedging all bets, a strip of card bearing the legend *'Trust in God'*. The driver's view was necessarily limited as a result, which may have accounted for his cheery optimism. After all, what the eye doesn't see ....

Within the depths of the truck the passengers sat in silence, resigned to seven hours of swaying in meaty proximity to their neighbours, enveloped in a fug of sticky air thick with the reek of goat and chicken, palm oil and male sweat. Bunches of bananas and sacks of yams vied with trussed fowls and calabashes of palm wine for every inch of leg room. The one advantage of cramming twenty five people into a space designed for twelve was that you couldn't get thrown about by the movement of the truck no matter how deep the potholes.

From time to time, as the poda-poda came to another bridge, the driver would stop and order all the passengers out. We had to walk across in single file. No-one looked down. Then, by death-defying inches, he'd edge the truck over. We held our breath as the planks creaked. Beneath the tyres another layer of wood crumbled to powder. Larger pieces broke off and tumbled into the foaming gully below. All around me people muttered what sounded like prayers in Limba and Madingo and Foulani. Eventually the truck would make it across and we'd all climb back in.

The accident happened as the driver tried to negotiate a particularly tricky set of ruts. We might have got away with it, except that the load on top of the truck was as high again as the vehicle and thus had raised its centre of gravity. The poda-poda swayed drunkenly and began to slide until, in a last terrifying lurch, it toppled sideways with a splintering crash. Bodies and benches were flung higgledy piggledy through a shower of yams and bananas. Women screamed, men cursed, babies shrieked, chickens flapped and squawked. The panicking goat emptied its bladder. A few people managed to scramble out over the tailboard and thence helped to pull others free. Winded by the large lady who had broken her fall on me, I was in turn pinned against two men in a position of quite indecorous intimacy.

It seemed like forever before we were able to crawl out. Miraculously no-one was badly hurt, only shaken and bruised. For a while we sat in the mud, surrounded by the contents of burst bags from the load on the roof. Among the casualties was one of my boxes of books, so that the accident scene was also littered with copies of Chinua Achebe's *Things Fall Apart*. Unfortunately no-one else could read English and, as I'd got no further at that time than 'Hello, how are you?' in any of the native tongues, it was impossible to share the joke. Consequently everybody else thought my helpless giggles were hysteria brought on by shock. The other passengers were kindness itself. While the men set about the task of righting the truck, the women gathered round, patting my shoulders, and I sat, like Job, being comforted – not with apples but bananas, and the gentle crooning of African voices.

Long Ago or Far Away

by Ian Cundell

The Luger automatic pistol was a lethal weapon in the hands of a ten year old. It could hold a roll of a hundred caps (tuppence a roll from the paper shop) and in the hands of a skilled user could wipe out an army of Germans. It was not so effective against a Viet Cong sneak attack.

Picture a row of shops, a paved apron with cycle stands, a phone box and a letter box in front, a battered service road behind and flats on the upper floors. Welcome to downtown Saigon, also known as the Five Elms Lane shops, Haven Wood Estate.

Graham was an experienced general and, seeing us move behind the Domestic Store's storage shed, had quietly led his troops through the Bushes and burst through the fence. A platoon of US Marines lay dead and had to count to thirty before getting up and re-entering the war.

We were well armed. As well as the Luger, Phil had a rather neat (albeit plastic) revolver, the barrel of which came out to allow a clip of ten caps to be loaded. David preferred the classic 'stick found in the back garden', which made a convincing Smith & Wesson. The rest of the army – Tony, Jim and Linda – made do with the two-finger pistol ('Blam!'), the two-fist Tommy Gun ('de-le-le-le-le-la!') and the one-fist-straight-one-fist-sideways Sten gun ('hu-hu-hu-hu-hu!'). By common consent, the Sten was an effective killing machine.

'We're in,' said Phil, finishing the thirty count in double-quick time. 'Where'd they go?'

'Round the front of the shops,' said Jim. I didn't say anything, since I was fuming that Kevin had shot me in the back without shouting 'Stop or I'll shoot.' That just was not on.

'Let's go,' said Phil. We sneaked along the side wall of the

Domestic Stores and Jim peered around.

Crack!

'Missed,' shouted Jim. 'They're behind the bottom wall,' he said.

The bottom wall was one of two architectural features, troughs in which various shrubs were planted, to add a little colour to the shops. Its mirror image at the far end was the top wall.

'We'll have to split up,' declared Phil.

His plan was sophisticated and clever. Jim stayed where we were, keeping the Viet Cong occupied. Tony, David and Linda disappeared through the hole in the fence, onto the access road for the garages at the back of Mum's house, allowing them to sneak up the back of the shops without being seen. They were to wait behind the off-licence.

Phil and I would flush them out. We slipped around behind the Domestic Stores and into the back entrance to the flats above. The front entrance was hidden from anybody behind the bottom wall, meaning you could sneak up on them using the Butcher's shop as cover.

As we edged along the wall Kevin's head appeared and he loosed-off a round from his silver Colt 45 towards Jim.

'Missed!' Nobody shouted 'missed' quicker than Jim.

Kevin hadn't seen us. Phil climbed onto the bottom wall and pushed the shrubs aside. When Kevin's head appeared again Phil fired. 'Gotcha!'

'Nah! Missed,' came the reply and we could hear the Viet Cong running.

'He's such a cheat,' I said. 'Shot me in the back just now.'

Jim ran to the wall and peered over. 'They're by the paper shop.'

We scrambled over the wall and took cover against the Butcher's shop window. Phil managed to work his way to the Wool Shop and covered Jim as he bolted for the Baker's.

Blam! 'Missed!'

We had to outflank them or it was stalemate. 'Cover me,' I said, 'I'm going for the phone box.' Phil fired two rounds from the plastic revolver, while Jim opened up with his Tommy gun. I screamed 'Missed! Missed! Missed!' and, swerving around the cycle stands and ducking, found cover behind the phone box. I could see their entire force. Graham, John and Henry had reached the Green Grocer. Anthony was near the top wall, but Kevin was pinned down at the Co-op. Revenge time.

'Cha-a-a-rge!'

Jim and Phil went after the main force, who ran and scrambled over the top wall, but I had only one target. I was faster, caught Kevin, put the Luger to his head and fired. 'That'll teach you to shoot me in the back.' Even Kevin couldn't cheat his way out of that.

The ambush was sprung as the Viet Cong tried to make for the back of the shops. We went around the top wall and when we passed the off-licence half the Viet Cong lay dead, caught in a hail of Tony's Sten gun fire, although Linda had been hit in the leg. She would have to limp for two minutes.

Graham had got away and Phil hared after him down the back of the shops, firing the last rounds from his revolver as Graham responded with his Captain Scarlet pistol. I paused to tell the dead Viet Cong that we were going to Phil's Mum's shed afterwards and rejoined the chase, the Luger blasting away.

And then – before the Provos, before drive-bys and drug cartels, when war was far away or long ago – I was stopped dead in my tracks. This is exactly what happened.

As I passed the back entrance to the flats a woman – she seemed old to me then, but was probably about twenty, maybe twenty-five – came out and shouted, 'Excuse me!'

Expecting a telling off for making so much noise, I offered an anxious 'What?'

'Are those real guns?' she asked.

It is forty years later and I have yet to be asked a more surprising question. And I no longer expect to be.

Euthanasia for Tortoises
by Frank Ferrie

The high wall that divided the front gardens and the back courts between the blocks cast a deadening shadow over all of us, but you could see white specks of dust and tiny insects floating in the air above our heads in the late afternoon sunshine. It was around five o'clock. One of the kids had found a dying tortoise. It was difficult to imagine; someone had just thrown it out with the rest of their rubbish. You hear about people tossing animals from their car, kittens and puppies, leaving them by the side of the road in the middle of nowhere and just driving away, but this was somehow worse. The kids had it on top of the midden, on the flat concrete roof, and were teasing it with sticks to make it move, forcing it towards the edge and then preventing it from wandering over. It was a cruel sight, the whole thing. You don't get much from tortoises: they look old and decrepit anyway, at least to the untrained eye; they hibernate; but this one was smeared in chip-pan grease, tea leaves and ashes from the bins. It had a wide splinter out of the corner of its shell and was hardly moving at all.

I guess you could call it a bravado thing, an act of defiance, 'late-summer craziness' – I'd safely say that now. But I think the rest of the kids were all a bit younger than me and my little brother was there. I wasn't used to that sort of situation. As far as I was concerned these kids were just fooling about with their little sticks, prodding the shell and swearing above their weight. I found a much bigger stick, a heavy one that had an enormous nail sticking out of the end and when I brought it back to the scene I felt momentarily triumphant.

That's when things got out of hand because the next step was obvious to everyone. I couldn't back off, especially after I had brandished the great nail a couple of times. I remember dragging the pointed tip across the concrete, feeling the surface in vibration, scrawling ragged white lines, procrastinating. I can't blame them for teasing me, telling me that I didn't have the guts to do it. But when they started chanting my mind became confused and my vision seemed all of a sudden blurred and broken up. I was curious about that; the crowd mentality and about what would happen if the nail hammered down on the little animal's back, whether the shell would break. For a minute it was as if those visual signals that the brain incessantly re-formulates into the bigger picture were breaking open, becoming distorted and flickering before the eyes, vision becoming emotion and vice-versa. But there was also a cold-bloodedness to my confusion.

I brought the nail down swiftly on the tortoise and it cracked open the shell. It took a few blows, I remember that, increasing the force, but what's strange is that I don't remember the wreckage of the dead body, just the blood against the grey, milky concrete and not much at that. There was that characteristic, rank, infested smell of the heavy steel bins, the damp ash in the air and ancient dishwater in my nostrils, but I must have blacked out the rest or maybe it simply wasn't that interesting. I can reconstruct it in my mind's eye, with my imagination, but I can't retrieve the picture-memory. I do remember though that it was no big thing to the rest of them. The kids just wandered off, one by one, looking for something else to relieve the summer doldrums.

My brother helped me to clear up the mess and put the wretched thing back into the bin from where it had come. We agreed that it was wholly regrettable and not to mention the incident again. I tried to cover my tracks further as we went up the stair; I ventured that if the tortoise was already half dead when we came along, perhaps I had done it a favour? But my brother didn't answer.

Threads

by Lesley Fuller

Purl one, creak. Knit two, creak. Pass slip stitch over, creak, creak – backwards and forwards she'd rock, knitting needles click clicking in rhythm with the groaning chair.

I wondered, as a child, did Aunt Bea ever leave it? It seemed to me then that she and that dark oak rocker were one. The chair chipped and marked by life, like Aunt Bea herself.

There she'd be hour after hour, an array of wool and twine, in dubious colours, threaded around her fingers, the chair and her days. The strands of her life woven into ours. She'd produce an overabundance of jackets, scarves, mittens, bonnets and myriad shawls for babies she'd never herself have. In turn the recipient babies would have children of their own, who, like their parents before them, were kitted out in Aunt Bea's often fanciful creations.

I remember a particular rigout I was made to wear – encased head to foot in a product of an Aunt Bea knitting frenzy. Matching leggings and jacket, socks and a 'tammy' plonked on my head to set the ensemble 'off a treat' said Aunt Bea. Being around five or six, I was only aware of how uncomfortable I felt, not the comments and sniggers. According to my mother there wasn't any, of course.

'We had to be grateful, in those after the war years, for whatever we could get,' she said.

Maybe she's right and many other kids looked as I did and daren't titter. But really! Green was never my colour.

That chair she had joined forces with, I've since found out, is much older than Aunt Bea. As a child, of course, I would never have been convinced that was possible – *nothing* was older than Aunt Bea! It had belonged to her mother-in-law, who she loathed with more passion than she gave to her knitting and so sat on in that chair defiantly, never being allowed this liberty when her mother-in-law was alive, despite the chair *and* her mother-in-law taking up most of the space in the tiny scullery of Aunt Bea's home.

A home that had a German bomb drop on it in the latter half of the war. Leaving Aunt Bea homeless and living with my parents, with hardly a possession left after the subsequent fire that engulfed the street. The old chair, though – it survived.

And endures still. Spending some years, after Aunt Bea died, relegated to the garage of my childhood home. My father would lurch and grate his way through his motorcycle manuals while employed on his latest 'tinkering' project.

The chair now resides with me, looking much as it did in Aunt Bea's day and yes, I know, I could restore it; return it to the once handsome chair it must have been.

But I like it this way – draft one, creak. Add metaphor, creak. Change the tense, creak, creak.

Coat

by Sue Gill

One rare moment of excess in my early life that I will never understand was bespoke tailoring. Although we live on a very small income, I am to be fitted for a new winter coat in dark green cloth, velvet collar, six buttons, pockets. A real indulgence for a four-year-old. Going to be measured is a delicious memory. Up steps to the tall town house in Albion Street; the fitting room on the first floor has two elegant windows and a hushed atmosphere. I stand very still while half a coat is put on me, then my sleeves are pinned into place by a stockinged lady wearing a pincushion on her wrist, held in place by elastic. Next she pins up the hem, moving round me on her knees on the carpet. I get a fizzy feeling in my scalp having this particular lady's body so near to me. It's lovely. I wish it would go on.

I am skipping out in the back wearing my coat. It's cold. Always cold. I am playing on my own, next to the coalbunker. Mum is in the kitchen getting the dinner ready. She comes to the window. It's time to go in. She knocks at the window. I look at her hand, the white knuckle knocking against the glass. There is no sound. I have become deaf.

Right now that's not a problem. I used to be able to hear. It's something wrong with my ears that's going to take a couple of years to fix. The no-sound knocking on the glass I register as absence of remembered sounds that used to be there. No anxiety. It's rather nice living in this dreamy underwater world. A world of touch and taste, sight and smell.

Every time the verandah warmed with the sun the perfume came back. Apples, definitely apples. Bill had built it himself, an extension to the little seaside cabin we women and children lived in to escape the bombs. Vernacular architecture of the hammer and thumbs school.

During the war the Canadians sent over boxes of apples for the undernourished British children. Proper storybook apples, half red, half green. Afterwards Bill got hold of the empty boxes – good strong wood – which he carefully took apart and lapped plank by plank, to make the lower walls of the verandah.

It was a place for my morning porridge in the heavy bowl with rabbits – or were they hares? – running around the flat rim to keep the porridge in order. No-one around, only the big reproachful horse looking out over the fence opposite. When we put the light on the startled silverfish ran about the floor.

I am mummified in a hospital nightie, trapped under starched planks of linen tucked in so tight that my feet are flattened. I have just had my tonsils removed to see if it will help with all this ear, nose and throat business and I will be in here for two days. The ward has the dimensions of a railway station. I can hardly see the grey ceiling. The opposite row of beds a distant horizon. I have no visitors.

My throat is barbed wire so I ask for a drink of water, but the nurse never returns. Hour after hour. How could she do that? She's hardly likely to mix me up with another patient. I'm the one with flaming red hair on the pillow.

Tucked up at my Nana's and still feeling bad, they try to coax me with a banana, a treat for the poorly girl who hadn't eaten for three days. I really tried to like it, despite its peculiar taste. It was supposed to glide down my tender throat. Concrete. Completely unripe. How were they supposed to know? Who had ever seen a banana before? I pushed it aside and closed my eyes.

One winter morning, I am putting on my green coat, ready to go out shopping, when Mum reaches over and opens the door. She has heard an alarming sound. It is an aeroplane about to fly straight into our house.

Actually it brushes the chimney pot and lands 150 yards behind us in the North Sea. There it is bobbing on the waves as we congregate with neighbours to watch. We stand in a single line along the cliff edge, looking at this huge thing that has descended into our midst. We are not used to surprises. One grey aeroplane, perfectly intact, tail towards us, floating so near. One or two brave people start tearing off their clothes, to swim out to it. I keep my coat on. How is the pilot? Did he survive? Looking back I realise I have no idea how the story ended, nor do I know if the plane was English or German.

Spread a sheet over the sofa. It's 1945 and there's no beds to be had in hospital. Something is erupting in my ear and I need seeing to fast. The emergency ear operation has to be at home. Chloroform dripped onto lint in a kitchen sieve pressed over my face by tall people in white coats. What are they all doing in our living room?

Aftercare ear syringing was done by the school nurse, when the warm waxy discharge would plop into the kidney dish on my shoulder. Leaving the school clinic one day, when all the others are inside at their lessons, I put on my coat and walk out alone across the empty playground and into the wind. I know a lot about wind. What it does, how it feels, how I feel about it, but what I don't realise is that wind makes a sound. When it moves the trees it makes a sound. I can hear the wind.

The Silence of the Children
by David Grubb

We are in Rwanda. It is late in the evening. We are waiting for the trucks to arrive. The trucks will not be filled with food or medicine or tents or water containers. They will drive into the place that was once a school carrying hundreds of silent children.

We know that they will come but we don't know when. We have water and biscuits for them. We have tents ready. We have a medical team waiting.

There are already hundreds of other children here. Most are asleep in the tents but some of them cannot find sleep. Sometimes a child suddenly starts screaming and an adult will rush to calm them, to help, to listen. That is easy. It is when a child is convulsed in silent screaming that one feels so helpless, so guilty, so utterly useless.

And now they trucks arrive. About twenty of them. The aid workers have found children hiding, running, sheltering in ditches, lying down exhausted. And dead children. Dead babies. And the silent children who have simply become lost, out of their minds, terror chilled; human fragments. It is almost as if they cannot see us as we lift them from the back of the trucks and walk with them across the yard or carry them.

And some have names. And some do not dare tell us their names. And some know who they are and where they came from and how they escaped the soldiers.

And others are stuck in a nowhere. They inhabit dread.

And as they lie down in a tent some lie down to die and in the early hours, when it is very cold, their bodies are taken out.

Those who have survived the night wake up to eat and drink

and wash and put on new clothes and there are adults talking to them and older children to help find out who they are and where their villages were and how they came to be alone. During the coming days some will tell their stories, some will draw pictures, some will act out their experiences. And there will be others who cannot do any of this. They have to be fed and dressed. They are not interested in the singing and the games and the skipping. It is as if they still see and hear other things. Even the older women who come to the camp to help cannot get through. No song. No laughter. No toys. No bright colours. Silent hours and days and nights.

Here is a boy drawing his house that had been set alight. Here is a girl using dolls to show a doctor what some men did to her. Here is a boy who runs about and he has become like an animal as he darts and scampers and tries to bite us. Here is a very young girl who will not wear clothes.
    Over there you can see the boy playing at football with others and then just when he might score a goal he stops, looks down at the ground, has lost sense of everything. And the game is over. What is game? What is play? What is anything? And no water, food, words can bring him back to us, can restore.

In another area there are girls who dance and there are children who have found old friends. There are children who help wash the babies. There are boys who help with the cleaning and cooking and keeping the tents tidy. And there are classes; reading, writing, chanting.
    There are stories to tell. There are ways to remember life as it once was. There are dances and small plays to bring back the colours. And each day some adults arrive, looking for their lost children. There are reunions. There are harsh disappointments. There are also some adults with other ideas; to steal children, to grab some of the babies, to take away.

And night after night they come. More trucks. More lost children. More babies. And also those who had become child soldiers. Who want to stay in hiding, who have lost face and power and are no longer children. They are taken to another part of the camp. They cannot be allowed with the other children. They will have to make an even longer journey back. They may still be dancing with demons. What is night, what is day for them? Why are they here?

Here is a boy in one of the classrooms who is telling the class about how he loved his parents, the animals they kept, the school he attended, the way the soldiers came, how the soldiers cut his hands off, how the adults were killed, how they remained in the ruins of the village and then walked for days and days and into the forest deeper and deeper and when it was totally silent they remained and lived off berries. And at night they heard animals but were not afraid. And after many days they did indeed begin to act like animals and look like some animals as they searched for water and anything they could eat and made shelters and some became sick and some ran away and some died and the forest got darker and darker day by day and sometimes they even thought that they had already died. And sometimes their parents were there with them, and grandparents. And sometimes animals that they had never seen before.

Here is a boy telling the class. Then others tell their stories to prove they are still alive.

And the moon comes here. And colours. And names. And toys. And games. And when it rains they all run out into the central yard as if it was a miracle. Even some of the silent ones because the rain brings back memories.

And the singing is about who they are. And there are moments when there might be more to come. And they learn what you

can do even when you have no hands.
　And trucks no longer arrive.
　And when they are dancing they are themselves again.
　Some are reminded of the proverb;

> I AM
> WHEN I
> AM
> DANCING.

Prospectors

by Tamara Guhrs

'But what are they for?'

'I told you: they're looking for oil.'

'But why are they doing it in the rainy season?'

My sister is full of questions as we walk up alongside the big yellow machines. There are creatures here we have never dreamed of, much bigger than the tractors and combine harvesters we've seen at the farm. These are serious beasts, designed to cut swathes through bush, and to probe kilometres deep into the earth.

'They can't do it in the dry 'cause that's tourist season. The tourists are here to see elephants and lions. They don't want to see great big pieces of earth-moving equipment cutting through the forest.'

'What happens if they find oil?'

'It'll be good for the economy.' It's the first time Jimmy has spoken. His answer is short and has a shuttup tone to it.

'We'll just pray they don't,' says Mom.

I know what it'll mean. No more of this. No more pale yellow grasslands dotted with zebras. No more *mopane* trees stretching up over the hills and into the distance. It'll mean money, which means people will come and fight over it, and we won't have a safari lodge any more, and we will watch the earth being cut up and those long metal poles ramming down into the red soil and black plumes of smoke vomiting into the air. My imagination flies forward to a time when the whole landscape is blackened and only a few smoky holes remain on the charred ground.

'It won't be pretty,' I say to my sister. I'm learning to talk like the grown-ups. To keep things short and understated. That night I do pray. I pray that if there is oil down there, the earth will hold on to it tightly, keep it locked up like a secret.

On Saturday Jimmy is in high spirits when he pulls his cranky old white Landcruiser to a stop outside our kitchen. Mom has packed cold water into the cooler box. She throws in the camping box too: the black pot that no-one tries to scrub back to silver anymore. A quarter of a bag of mealie meal, some *kapenta*. A loaf of bread. We're going on a Day Trip! Day Trips are a rare treat. They mean going further than Chichele Lodge, further than Lupunga Spur, further than the Salt Pans, even!

The Oil People have cut a Transect Line through the mopane forest and up to the escarpment. We're going to drive up their Transect Line. First, we pass the Airstrip, where they are camped. Long trailers parked in a semi-circle. You're not allowed to camp in the National Park but it seems that with the Oil People the normal rules don't apply. You're also not allowed to cut down trees. When we made a road to the bush camp we had to follow the natural curve of the path, drive around the tree, and bend left for two kilometres to where the river is easier to ford. The Transect Road is straight straight straight, and they've put little blue flags along the way to mark it out. Not that you can miss it. One of the big men steps out the trailer and we slow down. They've come to the end of their season, they say. The big rains are coming and they won't be able to carry on. They're having a party in the evening. Everyone's welcome.

Woohoooo! Wind in our hair as we stand up on the back of the open Cruiser, and our arms open wide so that you feel like you are hugging a big cushion of air. The speed limit in the National Park is 40km an hour but Jimmy is pushing it 'cause the road is so straight, and there are no animals up here in the hills.

We stop for lunch and make a fire, cooking *nsima* in the blackened pot. One of the trees that was chopped is bleeding great big globs of red resin. My sister and I scoop it up and make fake wounds on our legs: look Ma, I'm injured. Don't cry wolf.

On the way back Jimmy drives even faster, and leans out, one arm stretching out the side of the flying car, plucking the little blue flags as we pass. Mom doesn't like this – it's dangerous – but we squeal with glee as the pile of blue flags grows. Trophies from the Oil People.

The sky is pink when we get back to the Airstrip. They've put out a long long table and there are crates of beer and we are allowed Fanta. The table has white tablecloths on it but they're really sheets. As we sit there and it starts to get dark we hear the high pitched nipping yapping noise that makes your hairs on the back of your neck stand up. Wild dogs! They pass right by, trotting neatly, following a scent trail. A nightjar dips over the table and in the distance an impala barks. The grown up say things like Another hard day in Africa and It's Tough in the Tropics.

Then the lights come on: they've got florescent tubes and spotlights all rigged up to a big generator, and that's also how they run the video and TV. After dinner we all get to watch videos. Me and my sister on the one big couch, and Big Ben on the other side, next to her. The video is *Rocky*. Halfway into the film my sister leans over and whispers in my ear, Ben has got his hand on my panties. I whisper back, Take his hand and move it away. She does and he laughs and drinks more beer.

Later he does the same to me and I feel the same thing she must have felt – a frozen feeling, like not being able to even shout, only whisper. The flying ants smack against the florescent tubes and Sylvester Stallone sweats and sprays blood in the air.

On the way home, we are quiet, and Mom sits next to us on the back seat. I want to cry, I want to tell her, but something inside me knows, that it's best to keep it locked up, like the earth keeping the oil secret, deep in its belly.

Belong

by Ursula Hurley

These barricades can only hold for so long ....

According to the REM song, the world collapsed early Sunday morning. That's wrong. It was Tuesday tea-time. Late winter. The window in our narrow galley kitchen was already a solid black square. Rivulets of condensation trickled down the glass, glistening silver in the new spotlights. I remember thinking how pretty they looked, like a zebra seen in negative. But that was before the world collapsed, when I still believed in the influence of a benign force that made patterns in windows, caused black cats to slink across your path, and butterflies to land on your sleeve.

The kitchen was all new. Years of cajoling on Mum's part had finally resulted in Dad devoting a large part of his meagre salary to having the deeply unfashionable dark blue cupboards ripped out and replaced by proper fitted units in light ash veneer. The walls had been painted in Hint of Peach and the whole thing finished off with a matching clock and bread bin from Marks and Spencer's 'Harvest' range. I thought it was amazing. I had always assumed there was a law against people like us having fitted kitchens, tiled bathrooms and tastefully decorated homes.

You couldn't blame my Dad for being cautious with his money. Not when you understood his background, the mire of poverty and squalor through which he had struggled. To him, this tiny semi-detached bungalow with its handkerchief lawn was a palace, and what's more, it was his. He was haunted by the memory of his father standing by the back kitchen table, complete with the open bottle of sterilised milk that was a permanent fixture of the household, begging Hilda (my Granny) for the money to go down the pub and have a single pint of Guinness.

Consequently, Dad refused to borrow money. He saved up for what he needed, no matter how long it took, and then paid for it in cash. He worked a whole year teaching night school to buy our first fridge. He didn't care if the lounge carpet was threadbare and the sofa clashed with it. People, not things, were what mattered. Why have a new three-piece-suite when you could take the family to France for a month for the same money?

Dad marshalled Mum's earnings in the same cautious way he did his own. She laid no claim to a clothing allowance. Dad said she would look beautiful in a bin-liner and thought no more of it. She bought no cosmetics, rarely went to the hairdresser. That was okay. Her smile was worth a million pounds. Dad was un-materialistic to a fault. Mum complained that they couldn't invite people round to our house because she was ashamed of it. Dad found this offensive. People didn't care about the state of the house; they came to see you, he said. Always make people welcome, and never apologise for the carpet. That's why they had no friends, just a long line of lame ducks and hangers on.

I was messing about with a tea-towel, pretending to dry up. It was already sodden and I couldn't be bothered to search out a fresh one. The drawers had all been re-arranged in the new kitchen. I stopped and looked again at the window. The zebra pattern was gone. Beyond was the shadow of next-door's garage, a darker patch in the blackness of the night. The beautiful purple-leaved tree that used to grow there had been hacked down, its stump drilled with holes and filled with oil. Dad was worried the roots might get under the house and cause subsidence. Dad was worried about everything. I was worrying about my biology homework. Despite a bad start due to left-handedness and untidy writing, school had identified me as 'clever' and England expected. 'A' levels were looming next year. There had been talk of Oxbridge. Every 92% test score left my parents to enquire anxiously after the other 8%. Every night out (and there weren't many) led to worried looks on their part and overwhelming guilt on my part. Right now, I wanted to be in Windmill with a pint of Dry Blackthorn and 'Losing My Religion' on the juke box. Mitochondria and adenosine tri-phosphate beckoned.

'You know we went to the hospital today with Dave?' Dad reached over and pushed the door closed.

'Yeah?' I knew he'd had a follow-up appointment after a visit to A&E with a bruised toe revealed tight tendons.

'It's serious.'

I had never seen my Dad cry before. Clear snot ran from his strong proud nose. He wiped it with a tea-towel but Mum didn't comment.

'What is it?'

'Muscular dystrophy,' said Mum.

That wasn't on the biology syllabus.

Dad was leaning over the sink shaking with sobs.

'Well, isn't there a cure?'

Mum shook her head and put a finger to her lips, indicating Dave might overhear. Through the dimpled glass door I could see the back of his football shirt, with No.1 Grobbelaar printed across his narrow shoulders. He was sitting in front of the television playing *Sonic the Hedgehog* on his Sega Megadrive.

'It's genetic,' said my Mum flatly.

This *was* on the biology syllabus. 'X-linked?'

Dad extracted a bundle of pastel coloured information leaflets from the tea-towel drawer. He scanned through and nodded.

'Am I a carrier?'

Mum and Dad looked at each other. 'There's a test,' said Mum. 'If you want ....'

I looked at Dave, swapping cartridges from *Sonic* to *Alex Kidd*. I went into the lounge and knelt down behind him, wrapping my arms around his little chest, resting my chin on the back of his head, feeling his warm silky hair against my throat. And all the time, the lyrics of 'Belong' were running through my mind:

She held the child and whispered
with calm, calm; belong

Stickers

by Paul Jenkins

We were sat in the back seat of my uncle's Ford Cortina. Outside there was a storm and my Dad had run inside the hospital to see if our Nan was awake. It was a strange hospital, very quiet. No one was running about like they did on the telly. My Nan had been awake when we'd seen her the week before and I'd sat on her bed and asked about her eye and when she was coming home and we talked about school. We ate loads of grapes and my Granddad insisted on driving us back. It was a quiet journey.

Now I was telling my Mum about my day at school. She'd asked me but she was worried about something else. I could tell that much.

'Here's your Dad.'

I glanced outside and saw my Dad and his brother running towards us. They were soaked; even their faces were drowned. They clambered breathlessly into the front of the car.

'Nana's not up to visitors today, mate. We're just, you know, going to drive home and we'll sort something out. Okay?'

My Dad was turned towards us from the front seat and trying to address each of us at the same time. I was upset; I wanted to see my nana. We drove home, the windscreen wipers struggling all the way with the weather. By the time we got back my sister and I were both asleep so we were carried up to our bedroom at the top of the house.

Dad was gone all the next day. He'd left pretty early even though he didn't work Saturdays. Mum didn't seem to know where he was, just out. But he'd left a present for me and one for my sister. My sister had a doll and I had a sticker book.

I didn't know anything about football except it was what my friends now did at playtime. We didn't play superheroes or Top Trumps anymore; all my mates played football with a bright orange ball that belonged to Graham Broad who hated losing and had his initials painted on the ball. I used to read comics in the corner instead. Occasionally the ball would ping its way towards me and I'd try to join in but I was rubbish.

If it was raining and we had to stay inside then football still dominated proceedings – all the boys bar me had a sticker book and spoke dementedly of swapsies and gots and needs.

Now I had a sticker book with loads of teams in it and ten packets of stickers to start me off. When I'd finished putting all the stickers in, my Mum sat us down on the sofa and said she had something to tell us. I knew what she was going to say because she was crying. It was the first time I'd ever seen her upset. People only cried on telly when people died.

It was my first dead person and it was my Nan. My Nan who looked after me at weekends and gave me 10p to spend on sweets every time she came down and said 'Presently' instead of 'In a minute' and who had a plastic chair in her bath. I cried for as long as it takes a seven-year-old to cry themselves to sleep.

We didn't see my Dad till the next day and we didn't get the chance to say goodbye. We had a couple of days after the weekend off school and then when we went to school on the Wednesday my mum spoke to my teacher, Miss Hope.

I'd been quiet, quieter than normal. I could see the teacher and my mum looking at me in that way that parents sometimes look at children when they're ill.

I had my sticker book and my swapsies in my little Gola bag ready for playtime. Graham Broad had forgotten to bring his football and so the two of us and some other boys formed a circle like Chinese gamblers do in films. The names being read in some solemn incantation as the swapsies were announced.

Joe Jordan. Ray Wilkins. Bristol City. John Wile.

And along with the incantation came a mumbling chorus of declarations from the marketplace. Got. Got. Need. Need.

My eyes stung as I looked down at my stickers and realised I was speaking the mantra too.

Got. Got. Need. Need. Need.

Jon-Paul

by Freda Love Smith

I got home late and Jake put his arms around me. He held them there a long time, and I liked it. Now this is a hug, I thought. Then he told me that Ross found Jon-Paul dead in the morning. Oh my god, I said, is he going to be okay?

Jake didn't say anything.

No, no, no, no, no, no. He isn't, I said.

My heart – it is always my heart – waited to beat. Like the kind of drummer Dale loves. He told me years ago about waiting until the last possible moment to hit the snare drum. Behind the beat, he said, but still on the beat. My brother, on the other hand, says it's the exact center you want. He was born on May Day and is always after some ideal. Right in the pocket is what my brother says. Me, I'm never in the pocket, never in the centre. It's time to accept that I never will be. Not on drums and not in life.

Anyway, that's the way Jon-Paul drummed. Right in the pocket. The centre would move and he'd move with it. Somebody said most drummers are rocks but Jon-Paul was water. I didn't think heroin would kill him, I thought he'd always find a way to move with it.

The phone rang. I knew it would be Mindy. She heard my voice. You already know, she said. I sat on the couch and we both started crying. She was in Little Rock. I was in Nottingham.

But he was clean, we said. He'd been straight for months. What happened?

Later Mindy told me he'd been out the night before with Ross and Steven.

Steven, I said. I heard the way I said his name. How many bodies has *he* stepped over?

Sit down, said Mindy, just sit down.

How did she know I was standing up? She is in goddamn Arkansas and she cannot make me sit down, I thought.

I said one word at a time. Steven. Is. A. Spider. I will pull off his legs so help me I will kill him if he gave Jon-Paul drugs.

And what was my heart doing then? I didn't have a human heart. It turned into a lizard heart and I had a lizard brain to go with it. Lizard brain has three choices: fight, fuck, or run. Jon-Paul was dead and I wanted to fight.

It's easy for him, I said. He's never the one who dies. Fucking Steven.

Freda, said Mindy. Freda, she said. Freda.

I sat down.

Jon-Paul's emails had been manic for months, since the miracle cure in Mexico, and I didn't answer most of them. He said he felt alive for the first time ever in his life. But what can you say to someone who says that they are alive for the first time in their life and it's the tenth time in three years they've said this. What can you say when you've become afraid to be close to someone because you don't know who they are, you don't know which version you're going to get. And what can you say when someone tells you your friend is dead, and you realise that you'd been waiting for him to die, that you'd been expecting it, wondering when it was going to be. And that somewhere, way in the back of your mind, the thing you said was:

So he's finally dead.

The Cigarette Girl
by Liz Martinez

It was the seventies. You could get away with promoting cigarettes in that brazen, overtly sexual way. Red high heels, painted nails, long blonde hair, sensuous smile – a man would need a smoke after fighting his way past that.

My father was in court over it. He managed the shop. My father did what he was told; allowed the cigarette girl in, arranged her at the point of sale alongside the chewing gum, chocolate bars and other irresistibles for the impulse buyer.

Nobody saw the cashier. She was dull by comparison. Dark, angular and perfunctory, not sweet and smiling like the last one, and nowhere near as exciting as the red cigarette girl. The cashier's hair was short, like a man's. She didn't look pretty. But that was no excuse for not noticing her.

The tills in those days were great clunking safes with rows of big buttons. They made a satisfying sound as they rang up the money. They didn't work out the change for you. You had to know your maths to work one of those. You told the customer how much to pay, they handed you their money, and you counted their change back into their hand. I marvelled at how clever the cashier was, counting it forwards and then backwards again. She did it so fast. The cigarette girl didn't have to count. She just smiled and smoked, flashing nails, teeth and lipstick. The buttons on the till would have broken those long nails. The cashier's nails were ugly, short and bitten, like mine.

I loved the quarterly stock-take. The shop shut early on a Thursday afternoon. People still knocked at the door and peered through the window, even though the lights were off. My father took everything off the shelves, I wiped with a duster, then he counted everything back on, writing tiny numbers in long columns in the wide, blue book with the floppy plastic covers. I helped with the cigarette packets, stacking them neatly, pretty in their different colours, ordering them according to mildness or strength, 10s or 20s. I knew all the names and their proper places on the shelves behind the counter.

It was during the stock-take that they found the mistake. At Head Office, they told the Area Manager. He was a friend of ours. He'd been to dinner at our house. My mother had cleaned the house from top to bottom, and cooked a special meal for grown-ups only, with prawn cocktail starters, and boeuf en croute, followed by dark chocolate mousse and a glazed fruit tart. He even brought me a big box of jelly-babies. But he didn't tell my father what they'd found. We went on holiday for a fortnight, and when we came back there was another stock-take, straight away. They found it again, the missing money, even whilst he was away, but it was still his fault, they said.

Across the street there was a detective. He must have had a hidden camera in his bow-tie or secret binocular glasses, or maybe he hid around the corner with a periscope, because we didn't see him watching, spying on us, the manager, his children, the cashier. We were laughing with the cigarette girl.

In her evidence the cigarette girl said she hadn't noticed anything untoward. For weeks she had stood overlooking the till, poised at the point of sale, selling cigarettes. For weeks she had chatted up the customers and made polite conversation with the cashier, as the cashier rang up the goods, and then some more, took their money, counted their change backwards, and pocketed the difference. Day in, day out. All stuffed in her pro-thief bra. Balanced tills each night, happy customers, happy staff, happy cigarette girl every day.

The cashier was laughing, everywhere except on her plain, dark, angular face. The cigarette girl smiled, attentive and interested, everywhere except in her non-mathematical brain. My honest, hardworking, generous father was found negligent. His Area Manager gave evidence against him.

The Point Of A Pendulum
by Liz Martinez

I am shopping for a new pendulum. I already have one, on a thick string, from a witch in Whitby who used to do my tarot cards by phone. It has a Whitby stone with a hole in the middle, which she picked up on the beach and sent to me. The envelope said; *Careful – Wobbly*. I was thrilled. It felt wild and wonderful, and I was very young.

I like the idea of a witch on a windy, northern beach searching for my stone. I imagine her fingers, knobbly as the weather-worn pebble she chooses, shaking a little as they thread the twine through the hole, and pull it tight in a lumpy knot. Maybe she trimmed the string for neatness. Maybe she held the stone for an extra moment, to imbue it with her love, before sighing as she placed it in the padded envelope, sealed the package with brown masking tape, and wrote her warning to the postman.

A week from now, in a hotel on Miami Beach, I will begin to study the skills of the spiritual healer. I have enrolled as a student at the world's leading healing school, but they won't let me in unless I have the right pendulum. They're very prescriptive. A wobbly one from Whitby won't do it. The one in the diagram is pointed, for precision.

I have just one hour. I should be at work but someone told me there's a shop in Fulham which sells them, so I've snuck out for lunch ....

Later, at home, I kick off my court shoes, and pour myself a glass of chilled white wine. I rummage through my handbag for the brown paper bag scrunched around my new pendulum.

The wood feels cold. The smooth, grain-patterned surface testifies to the skill of the craftsman who turned it; it has a point. It is perfectly proportioned. I put my finger through the loop of its thin, cotton thread and wait for movement. Does it sense me? Will it want to work with me? Why won't it move?

Maybe I should ask it something.

'Show me YES,' I command. The motionless pendulum points at a stain, directly below it, on my carpet.

'Okay, then, suit yourself, show me NO.' Nothing.

'Have I offended? Was it something I said? Don't you like me?' Ah, now we're moving, left, right, left, right, left.

'Is that yes or no?'

And now, as I am settling in to my training at this revered and rigorous school, the initial tensions of our healer-pendulum relationship have eased. Like surgeon and scalpel, we have merged and we work as one.

There is a body on the table before me. I stand, bare feet rooted to the floor, knees bent, pelvis tucked in. I feel the familiar hot energy flowing up my back, and sweat running down my neck, although the air-conditioning is set to HIGH. Suspended from my finger, the pendulum rotates in a counter-clockwise elliptical motion, skewed right, over my patient's second chakra. At its greatest, the range of movement is three inches long. I turn to my patient's record and write 'CCER3', technical notation reflecting the precision of our healing science.

I return to my patient, and through the wide ocean-front window, I catch the view of Miami Beach. There is a woman walking. She wears a wide sunhat and her long skirt flaps against her legs in the breeze. Watching her make her way along the beach, I slip my hand into my pocket and grasp the knobbly stone that is hidden there. I wonder which way the wind's blowing today in Whitby.

Crows in the Toilet

by Alison McNaught

I am in my Nana and Grandpa's bathroom. I can smell the disinfectant from the hard, shiny toilet paper. I had forgotten about the crows when I sneaked in and locked the door.

Sally and Catherine live in the bathroom but I've sent them away, to help my Grandpa. I am upstairs on my own sitting on the toilet. The crows will be set free when I flush it.

To escape, I have to reach the bathroom door, and I have to unlock it and it might not unlock, and then the screeching crows will fly out of the toilet bowl and they will peck my bottom and that will hurt and no-one should see your bottom.

I shouldn't even be in here. During the day my Nana says I should use the downstairs toilet. But it's cold and it's down a long passage and out the door and you can't even hear the voices from the kitchen. There is a red floor the colour of blood in there, and the walls are whitewashed to cover the mould. And it echoes. It smells like when you've been sick and they bring a bucket out to clean it up.

There are no crows though. Only spiders that run sideways across the floor, as large as sparrows: they will use your legs for a ladder to climb into the toilet.

Upstairs is definitely better, apart from the crows.

The wall behind the table opposite the toilet has wild geese on it and long tall spindly trees growing out of a pale blue-green lake or sea. It makes you feel that it is somewhere no person has ever been. A place where birds fly and no-one is there to hear or see them. I know I would not like it there.

Next to the table is the door and my way to freedom. It has the key in the lock.

'Don't lock yourself in,' my Nana always tells me. 'Remember what happened to poor little Sharon that day.'

I did remember. I hated hearing my big sister cry. Grandpa had to release her by passing a sheet of paper under the door and telling her to take the key out of the lock and drop it onto the paper.

I want to cry now.

If I put the lid down the crows won't be able to fly out, but they might fly out before I can get it down, then I would be facing them and they would peck my eyes, which is probably a lot worse than having your bottom pecked.

I am brave. I take a chance. I slide off the toilet seat, slam down the lid, pull up my knickers and trousers, flush the toilet. No time to wash my hands. I run to the door, twist the key in the lock, which turns first time.

I am free.

There is no sign of the crows. But my heart is beating. I wobble down the stairs. I hear the steadying tick of the Grandfather clock downstairs in the hall, and the voices from the kitchen.

Winning

by Moira McPartlin

He said I was useless.
He said I was slow.
He said I lacked determination.
He said I was 'too fucking nice to get anywhere'.

Breakfast porridge bubbles in the pit of my stomach as I turn into the tent-strewn event ground in the guts of the Scottish Borders. I scan the field for a distinguishing feature to pitch beside and grab a spot, not too far, but not too close, to the row of blue Portaloos standing sentry at an open farm gate. What am I doing here in the middle of nowhere? Silly old woman, I should be at home making soup.

'Come on, you.' My club captain gasps as she bounds towards me. 'Your staggered start time is in thirty minutes.'

My throat cramps as I pack my bum bag with regulation gear, water and jelly babies. The last trip to the loo leaves me with the horrible sensation of needing to go again. On the starting line my heart pounds as my eyes devour each contour to figure out the best way to my first checkpoint.

At last the starter pats my arm. 'Good luck,' he says, handing me over to the mercy of the mountainside, alone, with my map clutched in my sweaty hand.

My calf muscles object halfway up the first hill; I put my head down and imagine my arms as pistons, pumping energy into my legs. I scrabble to find the first check mark, then I spot a girl in a white hat run from a stream junction; there it is, tucked under a stone.

Peat hags obstruct the direct line to the next checkpoint, but I know where I'm headed and I will my legs and lungs to stay with me.

The midday sun hammers on my back. The bandana round

my head is soaked, as are my shorts and running vest. My shoes strangle my swollen feet. The water bottle in my bum bag sloshes in time to my loping gate. I drink on the hoof and refill my bottle from the streams that I run straight through. Cold water kisses my toes.

As I top a gully the girl in the white hat crests the lip of the hill. I catch her at the edge of a wide river, where she waits for me.

'Would you take my photo?' She smiles, handing me a disposable camera.

'Sure.'

She's wasted minutes waiting for me, but I realise this is more than a race to her.

She passes me her route card and a pen.

'I'll take you; write your name and address, I'll send it to you.'

Stones and muck invade my shoes after the last checkpoint but I ignore the discomfort. Half a dozen runners struggle to ascend a steep traverse, but no sign now of the white hat. I slam some jelly babies into my mouth, and dig in.

I think of my ex-boyfriend who pushed me too hard, but I'm not doing this for him.

I think of my teenage sons who, like their dearly discarded father, think I am only good for skivvying after them.

I think of my dead-end job and the wee fat bully boss who believes that fear motivates staff. What's wrong with being nice anyway?

By the time I reach the summit I've overtaken five sweaty, gasping runners. Below in the valley, guarded by the line of Portaloos, lies the sea of green tents stretched out in ovation. I disengage my brain and take off. Knees bounce off my chin and arms flap wildly as I fly into the finish.

The photo arrives the next week.

Legs Eleven, go to Heaven
by Eithne Nightingale

'Amen.'

I open my eyes, my hands still together and look up at Miss Entwistle, our Sunday school teacher.

'Now don't talk to any strange men on the way home.'

My best friend Carol is sick today so I have to go back to the vicarage on my own. I don't really mind as it's not very far. Over the main road. Look left. Look right. Then past the bingo hall that used to be a dance hall. I can hear the man calling out the numbers.

'Eighty eight. Don't be late. Legs eleven. Go to heaven'

Those people won't go to heaven as they're not meant play bingo on a Sunday.

I cross the common, stepping over piles of litter. Rowntree's sweet paper, lemon sherbert wrapping and tiny rubber bags filled with goo lying limp on the ground. My mother says I am not to touch them. They are dirty.

As I climb the slope I look out over the bare moors. I can see the mills in the distance with their dark windows and tall chimneys that narrow towards the top. There is no smoke coming out of the chimneys because it is Sunday and no-one is at work.

I catch a glimpse of the vicarage roof and chimneys peeking above the sycamore trees. Nearly home. The Bishop is coming so we will have meringues and gingerbread men for tea. Mum cooks great cakes. Then I hear the sound of someone's steps on the rough ground. They're getting closer now and someone is running and out of breath. Pant, pant, pant. They are almost behind me now.

'My, my. What lovely long plaits you've got.'

Miss Entwistle said not to talk to strange men so I keep my lips pressed tight.

'My, my. What lovely red ribbons you've got.'

I know my new ribbons are lovely. They've got silver threads running through them.

'And what a pretty frock you've got on.'

Well it is true. My frock is pretty. Oh no! He's dragging me down the slope and I'm falling backwards. His hands are all over me – on my arms, my shoulders and on my chest.

He lifts up my skirt and pushes my legs apart, fumbling with his leather belt. For one moment he needs two hands to undo his trousers and I try to get up but his body traps me like a cage. I open my mouth but no sound comes out. And then it's as if I leave my body. I follow my voice to heaven where I can hear it singing with angels.

From heaven I look down on the little girl with long plaits and red ribbons in her hair, wriggling and screaming. I take a close look at the man. He has fair hair and is fat and stumpy. The little girl kicks out her legs so fast. Left right. Left right. Her lovely gingham dress is round her neck, her plaits swish around in the dirt and there are tears smeared all over her face. She tries to scream but she can't. And then it goes dark. It's as if the spotlights zooming down from heaven are switched off.

After what seems ages I pick myself up, pull up my knickers, brush off the dirt and make my way home. My legs hurt and I have to drag them along. I stop outside the vicarage, afraid to go inside. It is all so different now and I won't know what to say.

Then Mum comes out to the dustbins. She is throwing out the vegetable peelings from the Sunday lunch. She looks up and gasps as if she has seen a ghost.

'What's wrong?' she asks.

It's as if my voice has disappeared again. It's gone back to heaven. She takes me to my father in the study.

'What's happened?' he asks.

I still can't say anything. Dad rings the police. It only takes a few minutes for them to come.

We all stand in my Dad's study. Dad, Mum, two policemen, one policewoman and me. The policemen take out their notebooks and pencils. I stare at them and the policewoman asks, 'Is there somewhere quiet I can take her?'

My Mum looks down at the floor.

'You can use her bedroom.'

The policewoman sits on the bed next to me, picks up Sally, my doll and holds her in front of me.

'Imagine this is you,' she says. 'Show me where the man touched you.'

I look at Sally and I burst out crying. I don't want anyone to touch Sally where the man touched me. But I find a way to tell the policewoman what happened. About how I kicked my legs into the air so they touched the top of the tall mill chimneys. But I can't tell her what happened at the end. Someone switched off the spotlights zooming down from heaven.

My Mum bundles me into the bath to wash away the sins and dirt. I ask her if we can go and live somewhere else but she says, 'No. We live here.'

So I swish the water round the bath making waves. I close my eyes, scrunch up my face and make a decision. I will go back to heaven. I did not meet anybody there who was wicked to children. I will take Sally with me and introduce her to the angels. Yes, I will definitely go back there.

Dad Looking Sideways

by Amy O'Neil

I pull up. There's barely enough petrol in this old thing to get me through the day. I sit for a moment with dread in my stomach, delaying the humiliation. I'm outside the house where *they* are, the happy family.

Sometimes I don't know why I do it but here I come every fortnight – almost every fortnight. Once or twice I haven't been able to face it, but what does *she* expect with everything I've been through recently.

Anyway, here's to another day of not knowing what the hell to do and not having the money to do it, another day of their disappointment and my general failure.

I beep the horn.

Within a few minutes they come rushing out. The girls look miserable. Jack is more energetic, running and shouting something in his squeaky little voice.

'Hi Dad!'

The doors slam.

'Alright?'

I try to sound enthusiastic.

'So ....'

It's the same routine every time.

'What do you want to do?'

'Hmmm, don't mind.'

None of us have any ideas, but I guess it's good to see them. It just feels a bit forced, like I have to rack my brains for some activity to entertain them. They always need to be entertained. If I don't provide some amazing adventure then I'm a crap dad. They don't seem to understand the concept of *no money*.

I'm dying for some air.

I find myself driving to a garden centre again.

'How about Roundstone, kids?'
'Okay.'
The correct answer.

I just don't know where else to take them. Roundstone and Ford Market seem like the safest bets at the moment. The kids can just look around and play and I don't have to spend any money, as long as they don't get hungry or thirsty or see something they want.

The place is flooded with fairy lights, tinsel, shiny foiled stuff. Same old colours reappear, spelling out Christmas. I'm not afraid of heights but Roundstone gives me vertigo.
 'Dad, can we go outside and look at all the statues?'
 'Go on then.'
The water features in the garden are always a good move.
We walk around slowly. The air is freezing cold, but it's better than being in there, with all those sweets and sickening little Santas that smile at my kids and silently try to lure the last few coins out of my pockets.

I'm dying for a fag.

Annie's sitting cross legged, drawing a picture of a urinating cherub.
 'Wow, cool, Dad, look at that one, look at that one, Dad!'
They're temporarily distracted. Good.

The whole thing gives me a headache and no-one is on my side. My ex-wife just sits at home with my ex-mate getting fatter and fatter, passing off the kids for a day so they can have a cosy lie in, while I'm left to the impossible task of keeping them amused and playing the happy father.

I'm not speaking to my own Dad. I've no job, no money, no nothing; living with my Mother at forty. *Don't forget to smile!*

I take a deep breath of smoke through my teeth, and hold it for a while. Then I let it go.

After we've seen all we can see of stone gargoyles shooting water from various orifices, we head back into the artificial light. Jackie and Mandy annuals are all spread out on tables outside the overpriced cafe. Kirsten looks over but quickly looks back again. They've already got too many at home anyway.

I'm dying for a coffee.

'Do you fancy sitting down for five minutes, kids?'

'Yeah, can we go to the café?'

'Come on then, hurry up.'

The girls sip hot chocolate and Annie fills in the shadows of her earlier drawing. Jack has a coke. He's chatting so fast I can't even understand what he's saying; telling me about some new toy his new stepdad has bought him. The strong, bitter coffee stains my throat.

'Shall we go back then, kids?'

Kirsten spends the car journey sulking in the back because it's Annie's turn in the front. Jack is making fighting noises with two little figures he's brought with him. They're crashing wildly into each other, shooting, kicking and threatening each other in overly American voices. It's the loudest fight I've ever heard.

'Jesus, Jack, keep it down, will you? I'm trying to drive.'

He doesn't listen.

We drive back to my Mum's. It's before six, so I can still drive them back home in time for dinner. Sometimes my Mum makes it for them, or we get chips, but mostly I try and arrange to bring them back before so *their* Mum can deal with it.

We walk into a flat full of smoke. Mum and Bob are sitting in front of the telly watching an old movie. Bob is in his usual spot. He looks miserable and is smoking a cigar. He barely makes a noise as we walk in. I don't think he's said more than 'hello' to me in thirty years.

'Hello, love!' my Mum says.

She makes up for both of them though, talks for England and laughs her head off at old films even when they're not funny.

I'm dying for a sit down.

Jack's action figures resume their fight on the carpet. Kirsten sits with her Nan and Annie tears another page from her pad and starts sketching. I'm relieved.

Mum passes me the lighter for a cigarette I haven't got out yet. I take it and put it on the battered arm of the sofa for later.

We all sit together, watching the black and white drama on the TV.

Halfway through, Annie proudly shows me the picture she's drawn of my profile. I look bearded and old.

She's called it *Dad Looking Sideways*.

My Dad

by Clarissa Pattern

My dad is standing by the open bonnet of his car. The car is called Mr Henry; he's a green Morris Minor Traveller. I hand my dad the tools he asks for and my dad smiles and tries to answer all my questions. My questions are a long succession of whys. I can't stop asking why.

In ten years my dad will be dead. He will be gasping for breath. He will struggle to the front door desperately searching for air to fill his lungs. When I hear his screams I will think it is one of the greyhounds yelping from a beating. My dad will stumble around the hall surrounded by his family; his loving, useless, selfish family. I will ignore him for as long as I can. I'll stare at the unopened sailing brochure lying on the floor, the light bouncing off its glossy cover. I'll think of all the times I said no when my dad asked me to go sailing with him. I'll think of him smiling his wonky smile as he planned the holiday he could barely afford to take, asking me if I wanted to come, and me again refusing, no longer bothering to think of an excuse. I won't cry. I won't believe it. Then my sister's boyfriend will phone from the hospital.

My dad is leaning over the engine, fiddling with black greasy nuts. He's whistling while he concentrates on his work. I can't whistle. He's tried to teach me, but no tunes come out of my lips: only the sound of air molecules dancing in the empty air.

Sometimes my dad sits on the stairs and plays the clarinet, covering the sound of my mum's addiction to high body count action films with jazz tunes. My favourite song he plays is 'Summertime'. He sits on the biggest step and plays; I sit a few steps below him and listen. I silently sing the words in my mind, trying to remember them all and always failing. He's tried to teach me how to play the clarinet. I puff out my cheeks and sometimes it makes a screechy sound. I can read music though, but my dad isn't interested in learning what the notes look like on paper: he happily plays all the tunes that he's learnt by ear and I happily listen to them. Nothing else exists.

My dad is pouring oil into some secret part of the engine. I stare into the flowing blackness. There hasn't been any shouting tonight. No screaming, or screeching, or crying. I hate it when mum makes my dad cry. They argue about money, all the pets, the noise, the dirt, the smell, the television and other things I don't understand. It ends with mum in front of the TV and dad curled up in a ball, his whole body shaking. I write again and again in my diary that I hope my parents will divorce. We can all live somewhere with my dad and leave my mum to her animals and anger and mess. I ask dad why he stays with her; he says it's because he loves her. In a few years he will be asking me why he stays with her and I'll answer it's because he loves her and we will smile at each other.

My dad tries the key in the ignition. I am beside him with my fingers crossed. The engine rumbles a few times but nothing else happens.

'Ah, well,' my dad says as we clear away the tools. He pats Mr Henry on the side. 'We'll try again tomorrow.'

We walk back together down the uneven lawn towards the house, leaving the summer flies and occasional butterfly to enjoy the rest of their evening in peace.

The Edge of El Dorado
by Karen Phillips

We were in El Dorado. But there was nothing golden here. It was a shanty town crawling scruffily up the side of a mountain on the outskirts of Mexico City. Night was falling and it was rumoured that even the police had long since forsaken dealing with any callouts here. Rico and I were here in Fluffy-the-Van to collect a salsa band and their equipment from an El Dorado fiesta, but we had only just pulled off the highway into the town square and already a sense of foreboding was settling on our shoulders. Rico jumped down from the cab and heartily hailed a couple of shadowy locals for directions to the fiesta. Silently they pointed upwards. We followed the line of their fingers; a tiny road hair-pinned up the side of the mountain, disappearing into the deepening gloom. As heartily as he had asked, R thanked them and swung back into the cab commenting gently on the amicability of El Dorado's citizens. He gunned Fluffy's engine in a show of bravado and in a cloud of dust we hit the first hair pin bend.

Within about thirty seconds it became clear that whatever happened the only option was to keep going up. The hair-pins got tighter, switch-backing at eye watering angles, but there was no sign of a fiesta anywhere. Suddenly out of the dark, on a welcome few yards of flat road, loomed a cantina. It was the archetypal Mexican cantina, with swing louvered doors and a cluster of staggering men outside. Smashing bottle noises really were coming from inside. An unsteady figure grandly stepped into our path and held up his hand, and as we ground to a halt another face flattened itself against the passenger window. I smiled politely at it. Even from inside Fluffy, the smell of tequila and glue, the most widely available drug to Mexico's poor, was overpowering. With a motion for me to stay put, R opened his door and addressed the man blocking our path, matily asking where the fiesta might be. Quite a group was gathering, word having spread that there was a gringa in a van, possibly the first ever to be seen in the general vicinity of El Dorado. On realising this, Ric dropped the matey act and swiftly tried to shut the door again, an act complicated by the fact that two men were trying to get into the driver's seat with him. He managed to shove them off his lap, heave the door shut and we roared away. Now we were spooked. What was this place? When would this hill end?

We took the next steep uphill turns far too quickly, R panicking that the local mob would now be after us in a drunken rage, when suddenly, at the same instant, we both screamed. Screamed at the realisation that directly ahead of us was … nothing. No road, no bushes, no slope – just a gaping cavern of black space. Fluffy's brakes also screamed as we skidded to a halt and stalled, feet away from a vertical ravine. In our unheeding flight upwards we had missed a vital bend in the road and hit a tiny plateau at an improbable angle. On three sides of us was the dark drop of death. We sat there in silence, frozen with terror, the van creaking slightly. R cranked the door open and looked desperately around him, shut it again and asked me if I thought we might die. He restarted the engine, crunched into reverse, once, twice to be sure and released the clutch. Fluffy bucketed forward another horrifying foot. I made a kind of mewling sound. The only thing in my head was a half formulated prayer that consisted of two words – *Dear God Dear God* – repeated over and over, my fingers like claws in the arm rest. R was deathly silent, hunched and sweating, as he inched forward, backward, left, right, stones spraying over the edge of the gully. I lost track of time: I have no idea of how long Fluffy groaned and shuddered, impossibly blind and clumsy, but it felt like days – until *yes!* Tyres finally bit tarmac again at a happy angle and we revved joyously onto solid ground. From our new position on the final curve of the hill, we could see the fiesta lights a few hundred yards down the road. R sagged onto the steering wheel, wiping sweat from his eyes whilst I was assailed by an attack of hysterical giggles and tried to straighten out my clawed fingers.

From then on we entered a different world. Here was a parallel universe of fiesta, lights, hospitality, tortillas and *mole*, Bacardi and cokes, happy smiling people – and later, a surreally well lit and only mildly sloping road down a side of the mountain that surely – *surely* – hadn't existed earlier ….

Sometimes it's the Sound of the Telling
by Clare Potter

They move me up once a week to the big class 'cause I'm older. I like it but I don't like Mrs White. Her face is hard like ground. She shouts. Last week some spit came out and went on my book. So I didn't want to write on that page. She said, pointing in my back (my mam never points in me like that), *Why aren't you writing your words, Miss Potter?* And I said, *I'm waiting for your spit to dry off my page.* She grabbed my arm and lifted me into the corner. My feet came off the floor like when I dream I'm running in the air. She pressed my nose onto the cold yellow wall and said, *Stay there, naughty.*

Someone had poohed their knickers again. I could smell the steely smell and the smell from the rubber mat and the smell from the dough cakes we made last time. She shouldn't of done that to me. My arm stang. I wanted to go back in my class with Mrs. Abraham who sometimes cwtches us and gives me stories to write when I finish my clocks. I quite hate this teacher, though Mam says never to say *hate*. I think if she has a fight with my mam she'll win. My stomach swirls. Inside my mouth I say *I hate you, hatey hatey hatey hatey. I hate you.* Then I know I've said it out loud because there's wet on the wall from my words. On top of my head, there's a poster. I don't need to read it because I know it off by heart. I learn things easy off by heart especially my spellings for the week which smell tobacco-ee from Dad's tin. The thing on the poster is the prayer we say at the end of school: *Now the day is over, night is drawring night, shadows of the evening, steal across the sky.* When we sing that, I think of steel being sharp and cold and I think all kinds of things about those dark shadows stealing away the day ready to pounce on us when we are in our beds, like the cat that jumped in through my bedroom window and onto my face last week.

When I sit down, after I stick out my tongue to yellow Melanie who goes *ha ha* 'cause I been told off, Miss tells me to behave and that she doesn't want any more doings from me. On the wall is a picture of a Mister Man: Mr Chatterbox. He is a sort of square filled with pink crepe paper crumpled up and glued tight like the flowers on the embroidery Mam did when she was little. *See, children*, Mrs White says, spoiling my thoughts. She points that pointy finger to Mr Chatterbox. *That is Clare Potter, and Clare Potter* (she says this bit to me), *no one likes a chatterbox.*

She is smiling with her lips closed and the class is laughing.

I knock the smile straight off that ground face.

I'm not a square, I say.

Marianne, Me and the Giant Crustaceans
by Brenda Ray

When I was eight, Marianne was my best friend. Thin, nervous and highly imaginative, Marianne had a fine, almost poreless skin, very white teeth, and slightly protruding pale blue eyes that in time would become prawn-like. Her best feature was her hair, a shining golden blonde that fell almost to her shoulders in perfect corrugated ripples. Marianne lived with her tiny, garrulous mother and giant monosyllabic dad in a neat jerry-built pre-War house in The Lane, half a mile from us, together with the twins, her small, bullet-headed brothers, who were more eerily alike than any twins I've ever encountered.

Together we roamed the half-built housing estates, unfinished roads and ridge-ploughed fields between her house and mine, occasionally hanging about outside the paper-shop to read the comics displayed there. This went on until someone came out and told us off for messing up things we hadn't paid for, so we rarely got past the cover page. To this day, the exploits of Dan Dare and the dreaded Mekon will be forever incomplete. There were movie magazines too, and films were Marianne's speciality. Although there were still plenty of cinemas in the 1950s, it was seldom that I ever went to one, at least until I was over the age of ten. And I doubt Marianne did either. Her stories of the film world, and especially the truly tacky B movie, were handed down from relatives, notably her mother and a highly impressionable auntie whom I never met. These were duly related to me, then evolved into the plot of our ongoing two-person drama, The Game, which we played most of the time we were together, swapping identities and story-lines constantly as we strolled along. Lines like 'That leg will have to come off!', 'It's the electric chair for you, sister' and (my personal favourite) 'My God, it's ALIVE!' must have scared the pants off many a passing pensioner.

Marianne also introduced me to the world of popular music, which, coming from a Radio Three (or Third Programme, as it was known then) household as I did, was quite a revelation. And in those pre-Beatles days, also pretty dire. Marianne could render deeply embarrassing imitations of Lena Horne, Rose Murphy, Connie Francis and the dreaded Doris Day. Her very breathy Marilyn was particularly impressive. But it was the movies that were her true vocation, and although her corrugated blonde waves related more to Veronica Lake and the 1940s than the crimped styles of the 1950s, whenever I see a bit of Fifties Hollywood Kitsch, I never fail to think of her.

One day, outside the paper shop, we met Marianne's dad and the twins, and he bought everyone a Crunchie Bar. This remained in my mind, since sweets had just come off the ration and were still a great luxury. Not only did he buy one for all of them, but one for *me* as well. It was particularly memorable since Marianne's mother had never been known to give me *anything*, not even on the end of a pair of long tongs, so I felt doubly privileged. Marianne's house was in fact always closed to me, since Marianne and the rest of the family tended to open the back door very cautiously and peer round it before either letting me into the freezing cold 'glass-place' as they called it, or whispering 'Can't ask you in, we've got Company' or words to that effect, and shutting it again. I can honestly remember going inside Marianne's house just once, all the time I knew her.

Marianne's mother was very talkative, except to me, and had a slight, tight, permanent smile which seemed to have been pinned up at the edges and sprayed on with fixative. It was hard to imagine her, or her unseen sister, regaling the family, still less the ominous grandma with her bloodhound eyes and pan-scrubber perm, with sordid tales from the movies or impersonations of Doris Day, but according to Marianne, that was what they did. On the other hand, having a father myself who frequently aspired to grand opera with improvised cod-Italian (generally while shaving) or extracts from the repertoire of George Formby that were even worse than the real thing, perhaps I shouldn't have been surprised.

But as I said, movie plots were Marianne's particular forte, and what she didn't know, she invented with skill and panache. Many of the films she told me about duly surfaced on television and were instantly recognisable, but one has always evaded me. Recently, while clearing out a cupboard, I found a small folded map, drawn by me at the age of nine or so, of an island with various features marked out – forests, mountains and so forth, and intriguingly, 'Giant Crabs Haunt'. Suddenly, I remembered Marianne, eyes bulging incredulously, relating the unfinished (as usual) account of some obscure film set on an island inhabited by crabs as big as donkeys. Sadly, like most of Marianne's stories, it never came to a satisfactory conclusion, presumably the relative who'd seen it having fallen asleep at the crucial moment or rushed out to catch the last bus.

I often wondered what happened to Marianne, as by the time we moved on to secondary school, we developed different sets of friends, and her personality seemed to evaporate entirely. Schooldays over, I sometimes saw her tittupping down The Lane in wobbly stilettos and marked her out as probably somebody's secretary. I decided she would either marry her boss and live in luxury with a cream telephone and a downstairs toilet or run away to Hollywood and die of drugs or drink. I was amazed, therefore, to meet someone recently who told me Marianne had never left the village at all but married the landlord of the local pub. All in all, it's a pity that with her vivid imagination, Marianne never became a writer. But then, if she had, she might have sat down and written a memoir about me. And that's something I'd rather not think about.

A Bomb in the Airing Cupboard
by Joyce Reed

Green-apple paint and bright red knobs and very usual bathroom fittings. Subtle it ain't, but it's post-war austerity and I'm only five or six, and you don't notice what you've always seen. Outside, we're semi-detached – joined to number seven but separate from number three. The walls are done in little bits of chippings sticking to cement, and the shiny bits drop off all the time. Under the bathroom window there's a big, patched bit in the shape of a loaf of bread. There's a lilac tree in the front garden and raspberry canes in the back and nobody's allowed to touch those at all because they belong to my Nanna. It's her house and she doesn't share.

So I'm in the airing cupboard. It's very big and I'm not cramped at all. I had to climb on a wide shelf to get in. Banged my knee. And the ticking darkness holds the smell of warm sheets and Nanna's big knickers – why are they so big when she's so small – wasting away my Daddy says. And the blankets are all scritchy-scratchy on my legs, and the spare pillows are the lumpy ones we don't use any more. And the half incendiary (it's a big word but I learnt it) bomb is by my foot. I don't know why we keep it here. My Daddy explained how it would have worked, and why it didn't. It's fun to show it to my friends when they come to play. I bet none of them has a bomb in the airing cupboard. But mostly this is my place. I feel safer here. But I never quite close the door.

If I put a towel over my ears, I can't hear my Nanna and Mummy arguing. I want a baby sister like Ruth has, or a baby brother like Gail has, but Mummy says we shan't have one, not while it's like this.

And tonight Daddy has to go away again and I know it's

dangerous. He's a scientist and he has to find out why a lot of men died in a coal mine when it all blew up. When he comes back, his clothes will smell funny and he'll be quiet and tired and sad.

My bedroom's so cold that there are pretty frost patterns on the window. I trace them with my fingers and they melt away. I want to be warm in here, in the big cupboard. I keep thinking about the coal mine that blew up and all the children's daddies in there, and might it blow up again while my Daddy is in there?

I make a bed for Teddy with a few old flannelette cot sheets. And I listen, listen to the bus stop noises outside and the wireless downstairs. I just listen in the darkness, here but not here, hiding but wanting to be found.

The Journey Home
by Claire Riviere

A young woman who will one day be my mother is closing the door of a terraced house in a street behind Sloane Square. She places the key securely in her bag; she will not be using it for another week. In the chintz interior of an upstairs room a man ties up his shoe laces. Annette is in a hurry. People are moving around her but she doesn't notice any of them. She is no more than thirty, with dark eyes and auburn hair that at this moment is coming loose – the rest of it is drawn up with two tortoiseshell combs and her long dark woollen coat is flapping open revealing a round-necked emerald green jumper and a full skirt in a heavy woven fabric. She is carrying a black guitar case in her right hand and she has a small leather handbag with a metal clasp on her other arm. Every so often she has to stop to swap them around. Her eyes have begun to water. She slows down to a walk and then standing for a moment, she wipes the tears away with the edge of her gloved finger.

She continues past the newspaper seller who shouts out the headlines as he deftly takes money and hands the latest edition to passers-by. An old lady sitting on a wooden bench beneath the plane trees that are not yet in leaf notices Annette as she crosses the square. From her crumpled paper bag a shaking hand occasionally emerges and some stale breadcrumbs are thrown haphazardly onto the ground. The pigeons rise into the air as Annette approaches, they swirl around in front of the department store and then return to settle in a large group nearby. Heading south she goes by a flower stall with a canvas awning where a woman in a headscarf sits hidden by bright bunches of red, pink and yellow tulips. Then rounding the corner she vanishes into the mouth of the underground station.

Annette next appears at Victoria station getting onto a fast train. Every week she sits in the same compartment and usually she manages to get her favourite seat by the window. On the journey home she opens her book and places it on her lap but it remains unread; she lies back with her head on the antimacassar and occasionally turns to glance uneasily at her reflection in the darkening window. When she arrives home she greets the children who are nearly ready for bed. A shy Swiss au-pair girl hesitantly reports all that has happened during the day. Then Annette kicks off her shoes and settles down at the end of her eldest daughter Rachel's bed. Sarah and James sit on the floor wrapped up in a paisley eiderdown; they crawl around pretending to be monsters. The stories begin and they sit transfixed as their mother reads, her lilting voice carrying them to faraway places. Eventually she hugs each of them and turns the light off. Once downstairs she sets the table for supper in a mechanical fashion. Hugh, her husband, returns from work. She hears his car door slam and his footsteps slowly approaching the front door. He drops his briefcase down in the hall, removes his overcoat and taking his glasses off he rubs his eyes wearily as he peers at himself in the mirror. Annette greets him and he kisses her on the cheek and says he needs a drink. She tells him how her guitar lesson went but he's not listening. By half past eight they are sitting opposite each other at the white Formica-topped table. She lights the candles in their brass candlesticks and they drink red wine out of blue fluted glasses that she brought back from Venice. They talk quietly sticking to safe subjects like the children and the house and what changes they might make to it.

The year is reaching its end. Annette crosses the threadbare Persian rug and looks out from her bedroom window at the snow-covered cherry tree. A thick layer of whiteness covers the seat of the swing and the ropes look frozen hard. I am curled within her. I kick and she rests her hand on her stomach as if to comfort me. Soon I will be lying in the Victorian pram under the same tree. I will watch the fringed canopy sway as I am pushed across the grass and I will hear the distant squeals of Rachel, Sarah and James as they tear around the garden. I am born on the shortest day of the year while the doctor is out Christmas shopping. I share my birthday with Hugh who sits waiting in an anonymous room on the ground floor of the maternity wing. Later Annette says that having me was like shelling peas. I have jaundice but we are home in time for Christmas. I am a peaceful baby; I don't want to make any trouble. The days spent listening at doors and hiding in corners, of not belonging and not understanding, have not quite begun.

Reds Under the Bed
by Nick Robinson

Reds Under The Bed. Anyone remember that slogan? It was everywhere in the Sixties. Most of the Seventies too. They were out to get us, the Ruskies, the Commies, the Reds. Everyone said so: the Conservatives, Cold War novelists, my parents. Especially my parents.

No-one could have called my parents dumb. They were sharp, witty, bright. Dad was a partner in a successful accountancy practice; Mum had a significant job there too. They were first on everyone's guest list for parties, they had three healthy sons, a nice house in the country, so much going for them. So why were they so totally paranoid?

Somewhere, sometime, some dope had managed to persuade them that Britain was in permanently imminent danger of being invaded and taken over by the Russians. They had agents as well, the Russians: stooges and sleepers who'd infiltrated every British institution to prepare the invasion. The trade unions, they were full of them. So was the Labour Party, and as for the BBC, well, they were all a bunch of lefties.

Leftie was such a common epithet in those days: the Express and Mail labelled anyone to the left of Genghis Khan as a leftie. Students: they were all lefties, 'carrying on with one damn thing and another'. Trade unionists as well: all those leftie-inspired strikes. Whenever a high-profile union leader was interviewed, someone like Hugh Scanlon or Jack Jones, my dad would nearly choke at the sight of them. 'Nay, blood and sand, who the hell's this now?' he'd exclaim. 'Maureen, have you heard this? Disgrace they are, a bloody disgrace, holding the country to ransom.' Mum would agree, and woe betide me and my brothers if we dared say any different.

Heaven knows how long they'd had these views. As far back

as '67 they were convinced that the education system was under threat from the reformers and their secondary moderns, so I was rushed into the eleven-plus at the age of ten, and plunged into grammar school before the Commies tore them down brick by brick.

The country was 'going to the dogs' in those days; it was 'finished'. Forty years on I still hear people say that; it's kind of comforting. 'If we were younger,' I'd hear my Dad say, 'we'd be off. There's no future here anymore.' Where to they'd never say, and asking the question wasn't a smart move. 'Anywhere! Anywhere but this bloody place!'

So you're getting the picture? Don't get me wrong, there were lots of laughs, good times, plenty to enjoy, it was just that it didn't take much for this spectre of reds-under-the-bed to rear its head. Probably the most spectacular example this was in 1975. It's a memory that can still have me in stitches thirty-five years on.

Harold Wilson was PM and Tony Benn, the former Anthony Wedgwood Benn and Viscount Stansgate, was Energy Secretary. To my dad, 'Wedgie' was positively the looniest of all the loony lefties.

One Sunday morning, after church, Dad tootled off to the newsagent and returned with the Sunday Express. On his return Mum sneaked a look at the paper to check the TV page, and her eyes alighted on the programme scheduled for 2pm. The starkness of the listing caught her eye. It read simply: *Mr Benn*. 'Maurice?' she exclaimed. 'Maurice, have you seen this, what's all this about?'

Dad grabbed the paper. '*Mr Benn*? What the hell's all this? You don't think there's been a takeover, do you? Put the radio on.'

Mum tried the setting that had been the Light Programme before the Lefties at the BBC morphed it into Radio 2. Nothing. Try Radio 4. Nothing there either. Leave Radio 1, we're not having that racket on. 'Ring Denis and Jean, see if they've heard anything.'

Denis and Jean were out. Dad tried Alan and Olwen; they hadn't heard anything. 'Well, why don't we go up to the pub and see if anyone's heard anything?' I always thought that the writers of *Shaun of the Dead* stole the plot from us.

'Tony, did you see this in today's paper?' Dad enquired of the White Horse landlord. *'Mr Benn?* Have you and Pam heard anything? We were wondering if there'd been a takeover, a coup!'

'Wouldn't surprise me with that bloody Wedgie Benn,' said the landlord. 'He's a right one, him. Don't know why he doesn't go to bloody Russia if he likes them so much.'

The same question was asked of the regulars but they knew nothing, and only really cared about their pints of mild.

Mum and Dad never left a pub before chucking-out time. Never. And they stretched the drinking-up time to the limit, as well. This Sunday, though, they broke the habit of a lifetime and we all left at 1.45 to witness what they thought could be the darkest day in Britain's history.

'What time is it now?' Dad asked of Mum as we arrived home.

'Five-to. I'll go and put the telly on straight away.'

We all stood up to watch the start of that programme, like you might to hear about a terrible tragedy or the death of a Royal. Mum was more anxious than anyone: she actually brought her hand to her mouth as the announcer said it was time for *Mr Benn*. She lowered it

in disbelief as a musical refrain began. 'Bop-de-de-bop-de-de-bop-de-de-bop-bop.' 'Hello, children,' announced narrator Ray Brooks. 'Heeere's ... Mr Benn!' A bowler-hatted cartoon character hopped across the screen.

We tried not to laugh, me and my brothers, but it was totally impossible. We couldn't stop. Clutching our stomachs, tears streaming down our cheeks, I don't know how long we were kekking ourselves for. Even Dad joined in after he'd finished exclaiming 'blood and sand' and 'hell's bells'. When he looked again in the paper he saw the 'R' for repeat next to the listing.

It was quite some time before they dared to return to the White Horse.

Camping in France/En Famille
by Sylvia Sanderson

Wake up. The airbed has deflated itself *again* during the night. Why do I always land up with the duff one? Feel for sandals, negotiating the small rocks and boulders that litter the floor of the tent. England might be wetter and colder but at least you can be fairly confident of pitching on grass. Seventeen-year-old daughter totters into the parents' tent, still doubled up from sleeping in a small ridge pitched next door. Pausing to examine bites in camping mirror perched precariously on shelves above camp kitchen, she complains that we snored all night.

Husband has disappeared to join the loo queue so I heave up a four litre water bottle to fill the kettle. Someone has left the matches in a pool of cooking oil, I note bitterly. Moaning softly to myself, I search for the reserve box and come across the marmalade in the first-aid kit. All my careful planning is sabotaged by a family that refuses to understand that the secret of 'happy camping' is a place for everything and everything in its place. Realising that planning a family camping holiday is on a par with planning an ascent of Everest, I was determined to be better organised this year. I started with a list-list, if you see what I mean: food list; kitchen equipment list; cool box list; beach list; first night list and so on.

Then once the tents were pitched I put everything in the place assigned and explained my arrangements to my family. And what a waste of time that was. Sighing, I am about to start on breakfast when I discover that the gas has run out. Husband returns looking very self-satisfied after his ablutions (his awful word, not mine) so I despatch him to the camping shop to get a cylinder. While he's away I open the cool box to see how the war with the ants is progressing. The seal has 'gone' on the lid so every morning I find Flora, bacon, cheese, ham crawling with ants. Putting a boulder on top did no good so let's see if spraying the rim with fly spray did any better.

Mm. There's only one battalion inside and since I took the precaution last night of sealing all the food with cling foil, I feel the tide is turning in our favour. Wash the ants off the yoghurt and milk cartons, slice the bacon and clean out the box yet again.

'No. Breakfast is not ready yet,' to fifteen-year-old son. Nearly garrotting himself on the guy lines because he is eyeing nubile French girl doing her morning exercises, husband returns with the gas.

'Did you remember the baguettes?' Stupid question and it's my fault anyway for not reminding him. I unwisely take the top off the marmalade and then have to beat off cohorts of invading wasps. Connect up the gas and at last boil the kettle for a much needed cup of tea.

'What I want to know is who left the top off the sun tan oil? Look. It has dripped into the sugar.'

Son demands an aspirin and asks whose idea it was to come camping anyway and where's his socks and who left his swimming trunks out all night? And there's this insect in his trainers. He sits down with an angry jolt and the milk slides gracefully across the table and tips itself over the towel husband had draped onto the chair instead of hanging it on the line as instructed.

'Who moved that stone? If it had been left under the table leg, where I had placed it, the table would have been perfectly stable.'

The slope did not seem so acute when we pitched. Now everything is done at an angle of 45°. Every morning I awake to find myself at the bottom of my sleeping bag, a peg embedded in my thigh, wedged against the side of the tent.

Husband returns with the baguettes. He is pleased with himself, I can see. He calls 'Bonjour!' and, worse, 'Il fait beau' to our amused French neighbours and explains carefully to his bored and unimpressed offspring how he asked for 'quatre baguettes' at the shop and understood the reply *and* gave the correct price.

'What does he want, a round of applause?' mutters daughter, who is deep into split ends again. Fortunately husband is not receiving but off on another story.

'I was first in the washroom this morning, minding my own business, shaving, when in comes this French guy. He must have realised I was English. I can't think why.'

Looking at his shorts, Marks and Sparks tee shirt ... and his trainers, I can.

'Anyway there is this long, thoughtful pause. Finally and very slowly, obviously reaching back to schoolboy English, the Frenchman announces, 'Zee sun ... eez shineeng in ze ... sky.'

'What did you say?' I ask.

'Well there's not much you can say, is there. I just said "Oui".'

I smile. This holiday wasn't such a bad idea after all. The crusty bread tastes very good. The sun slants down through the pines. A delicious smell of newly ground coffee mingles with the warm Mediterranean scent of wild thyme. Perhaps I'll postpone for a day or two suggesting a package to Tenerife next year.

Strange Fruits
by David Craig Smith

'Unless a medicine tastes nasty it can't be doing you very much good.' That was a belief widely held back in the 1940s. Happily for me it was not a view that carried any weight in our house. My father was a pharmacist who would go out of his way to make each of my childhood illnesses as pleasant an experience as possible.

I don't recall the aches and pains or fevers that accompanied those infant complaints. I can barely remember the itches and irritations or the spots and pimples that must have been the symptoms of some of them. But I can still clearly hear my mother's admonishing voice repeatedly saying, 'Don't keep scratching or they'll never go away.'

What I remember best are the days of quarantine and convalescence, which I spent tucked up in bed whilst my less fortunate peers were tramping off to school. These were the days before central heating, when winter bedrooms could be chilly places. But my mother had the perfect remedy. She would take a shovel load of burning coals from the downstairs fire, carry them up the carpeted stairs to my bedroom and deposit them in the small iron grate. In times of health, irrespective of freezing temperatures, this bedroom fireplace would normally be sealed off by means of a tinplate advertisement for Camp Coffee. This had been given to my father by the manufacturer's representative and was intended for display in his shop.

As a prelude to transplanting the burning coals my mother would have stuffed old newspapers up the bedroom chimney. She would now set these alight 'to clear the soot.' The accompanying roar would muffle the sound of the wind buffeting the window. The clicks and gurgles of a central heating system coming to life, no matter how efficient, will never match the promise of warmth and comfort that was heralded by that explosive woof of burning paper. I would turn to the window and stare with delight as charred newsprint, some still glowing red around the edges, drifted from the sky and danced in the breeze like huge black snowflakes.

Now my mother would prepare hot milk, flavoured with cinnamon. This she would ceremonially present to me in a sturdy white invalid cup and I would savour the sweet, creamy liquid through the comfort of its gently curving teapot spout. This wonderful receptacle was only ever brought into use on these rare occasions and so, in my eyes, held equal status with my mother's best china, which was only seen at Christmas or occasionally on birthdays.

The doctor would arrive and take my breath away by placing his ice-cold stethoscope against my bared chest. His face would register mock amazement, panic and despair and finally relief before he patted me on the head and reassured me that I might just possibly live. He would depress my tongue with a spatula then set me the almost impossible task of saying 'aahh'. Then he would shake a thermometer, slide it into my armpit and ask me if I was yet able to count to a hundred. Finally he would extract his fountain pen from his breast pocket, unscrew the cap and write out a prescription.

I would have been heartbroken if he had ever failed to do this. That small rectangle of paper with its scrawl of hieroglyphics was for me as full of promise as a winning ticket in a raffle.

My father's shop was less than a quarter of a mile from our house, near enough for him to walk home for lunch. This meant that I did not always have to wait until evening for him to prepare the doctor's remedy. He would never do this in his dispensary. Always he would bring the ingredients home and mix the medicine before my eyes.

I would watch entranced as he spooned granules and powders and measured liquids in his conical flask, before decanting them into a bottle with an embossed measure running like a ladder up its spine. This could not have been a more enthralling spectacle if my father had performed the rituals dressed in a star-spangled robe and pointed hat.

Inch by inch the bottle would be filled, looking first clear, next pale and cloudy and then as rich and creamy as my mother's cinnamon milk. At this point my father would turn to me and ask, 'What flavour would you like?'

I was tempted always to say banana, believing these to be my favourite fruit. In truth I had never seen a banana, let alone tasted a real one. These were the post-war years and the importing of exotic fruits had yet to recommence. But I would resist and vary my choice of flavour in barely containable anticipation of the question that I knew was next to follow.

'Now what colour would you like it?'

The thought of yellow blackcurrants or purple oranges would reduce me to fits of giggles that made it almost impossible for me to reply. I probably derived as much benefit from this laughter as I did from the medicine when I eventually drank it.

Now my father would hold the bottle close before me as he dripped in the beads of richly coloured liquid. The magical drops would sink slowly through the solution, gradually dispersing like plumes of downward drifting smoke. Finally my father would seal the bottle with a cork and shake it vigorously until the whole concoction turned dandelion yellow, sunset pink, tropical green or vibrant ocean blue. Just the mouth-watering appearance of it could make me feel better.

Sadly, not all of the medicine would taste quite as nice as it looked but I never complained. How could I? What other boy had a magician for a father who could charm him back to health with green raspberry tonic, red lemon linctus or blue banana syrup?

A Bright Enough Lad

by Meic Stephens

Yesterday I received an invitation to address the Old Boys' Association of the Grammar School where I was a pupil in the early 1950s. After a moment's pause, and not without a twinge of conscience, I said I'd let them know tomorrow. But I find myself unable to make up my mind whether I should accept. I'm aware that, in my day, Pontypridd Boys' Grammar School was reckoned among the best in south Wales. It was there, moreover, I received my secondary education, thanks to the Butler Act of 1944, which made it free to all who passed the 11+ entrance exam.

But looking back – 'Say, can that lad be I?' – I see that the Grammar School was geared to turning out boys who, if at all academically gifted, were intended to leave their home patch, rarely to return, thus depriving the community of its most talented youth. I can name all fifteen Prefects in the group photograph taken during our last year in Form VI, but only two of us remain in Wales. Getting on meant getting out and the School motto, *Ymdrech a lwydda* ('Effort brings success'), was taken to mean just that. We left school with 'For export only' stamped on our foreheads.

Most people find something pleasant to remember about their schooldays, as indeed they should, and most reminiscences, like Tolstoy's happy families, resemble one another. I enjoyed my English lessons with Mr Ken Davies, who introduced me to Yeats, Eliot and Auden, and Mr Dennis Clare, who gave me his own dog-eared copy of *The Oxford Book of English Verse* as a prize for a poem at the School Eisteddfod entitled 'On a Welsh Victory at Cardiff Arms Park'. I even learned a little Latin from Mr Herbie Taylor, whose countless examples of prose style were meant to stand me in good stead in later life: 'The arrows of the barbarians will not frighten our men' – that sort of thing. Art lessons could be fun, too, because Mr John Whitehead, with his handlebar moustache a dead ringer for the comedian, Jimmy Edwards, left us to doodle and daub while he chain-smoked and brewed tea in his cubby-hole at the back of the classroom. Such men figure in most schoolday reminiscences and, sixty years on, even they fade among the grey faces peering from Staff photographs in the School history. Alas! I can put a name to no more than a handful and so would find it hard to speak about them as a guest of the Old Boys' Association.

It may be difficult to grasp now, but secondary school teachers in those far-off days belonged to the same professional élite as doctors, solicitors and bank managers: they had a status based on salary, education and a middle-class way of life that, in the Valleys, set them apart. Most wore suits, drove cars and lived in the posher, leafier parts of town where the houses had front gardens, bay windows and names rather than numbers, and their wives held coffee mornings and were members of the local Golf Club. The majority wore academic gowns, some even sported hoods, though in my time it was only the Headmaster, Mr P. R. Jones, known as Nap on account of his lantern jaw and a habit of keeping one hand inside his jacket, who kept up this tradition.

I have one fond remembrance of Mr P. R. Jones, which involves Al Johnson. It was shortly before the first lesson of the afternoon and Form IVB were waiting for our teacher to arrive and call the register. There was just time for some light entertainment and it was my turn to provide it. So I went out to the front, and going down on one knee, began singing.

'Maaaamy! Maaaamy! The sun shines east, the sun shines west ....'

The other boys watched as I clasped one hand to my chest, the other fluttering in the air and my eyes rolling like Al Jonson's, except I didn't have a blacked-up face.

'But I know where the sun shines best ....'

Some of the boys were standing on their desks and clapping and cheering wildly as I went through the famous routine.

'I'd walk a million miles for one of your smiles ....'

It occurred to me at this point that perhaps the others had begun to lose interest but I was determined to carry on to the crescendo, 'My Maaaamy!'

There was no applause except for a single pair of hands clapping slowly, irregularly, in mock-appreciation. The classroom was hushed and the boys were making sheepishly for their seats. When I looked up I saw what they could already see: Mr P. R. Jones standing, with his famous jaw thrust out, in the doorway.

'Stephens,' he said, 'come and see me at four o'clock. You ain't heard nuthin' yet.'

Astonished as I was to hear him using Hollywood slang, I knew only too well what an invitation to his study at four o'clock meant. I spent the rest of the afternoon in keen anticipation of six of the best.

'Enter!' he called when I knocked at the door.

The study smelt of fresh polish and stale cigar-smoke and there was a vase of gladioli on the windowsill. The Headmaster made a show of tidying some papers on his desk and didn't look up as I came in and, well out of reach of his right arm, stood shifting uneasily from one foot to another. When he eventually deigned to notice me it was with a weary sigh, whereupon he seemed to relax and a wan smile flickered over his stern countenance.

'Well, Stephens, it seems you're fond of the cinema.'

'Yes, Sir.'

'Mmm ... do you go often?'

'Yes, Sir, every week, Sir.'

'Mmm ... where do you go?'

'The White Palace, Sir.'

'Mmm ... and what films have you seen recently?'

'*The Count of Monte Christo*, Sir.'

'Mmm ... what about *Mrs Miniver*? They tell me it's good.'
'No, Sir.'
'Mmm ... what else have you seen?'
'I saw *Michael Strogoff*, Sir, when it came to the Cecil, Sir.'
'Mmm ... did you like it, boy?'
'Yes, Sir, but it was all in Russian, Sir.'
'Mmmm.'

The exchange of critical opinion between the two film-buffs didn't seem to be leading anywhere. The Headmaster shuffled his papers again and when the large clock on the marble mantelpiece struck the half-hour, stared at it as if in utter disbelief.

'Off you go, boy, or your parents will be wondering what's become of you.'
'Yes, Sir. Thank you, Sir.'
'Oh, and Stephens ....'
'Yes, Sir?'
'Don't let me catch you fooling about again, will you?'
'No, Sir. Sorry, Sir.'

It was a strange experience to visit the School a few years ago and see how small the Headmaster's study actually was.

My parents, neither of whom had had a secondary education, looked up to such men with all the deference of which the working class was capable. So it must have taken some courage for them to complain when I was thrashed by the Woodwork master, a man called Owens, for not putting my name on a wretched piece of wood it had taken weeks to saw, chisel and glue into the semblance of a toothbrush-rack. He hit me so ferociously with a steel ruler that I could hardly walk or sit down. I shall never forget how my father, still dressed in the overalls he wore at work, took off his cap as we were ushered into the Headmaster's study, where I was made to take down my trousers to show the weals and bruises on my back, backside and thighs. My parents were too easily fobbed off with an assurance that Owens would be cautioned, as maybe he was, for he sneered at me thereafter.

There were others just as brutish. The Welsh teacher, Mr William Lewis, known as Willie Woodbine, taught me only to memorise a nonsensical rhyme about going to Aberdare to buy a cockerel, largely by dint of cuffing me about the ears until I got it right. That was the sum of the Welsh I learned at school, and I dropped it in favour of French at the first opportunity, as bright boys were encouraged to do. It was to be many years before I learned Welsh and made it the language of my home.

I found the teaching of Welsh History confined to the luminaries of the Methodist Revival. We weren't even taught the national anthem – in the town where it had been composed. The History teacher, a Mr Parry, was a native of Blaenau Ffestiniog, and fair game as the butt of schoolboy insolence. One of my classmates used to pretend he had an auntie living somewhere up in the flinty wastes of the North and used the alleged connexion in a blatant attempt to curry favour with Mr Parry. It was he who had the job of fetching the master's newspaper and a large packet of Craven A from the corner-shop every morning, for which, we were all convinced, he was allowed to win the recitation prize at the School Eisteddfod on St. David's Day.

'Now tell me, boy, where did you go for your holidays this year?'

'Blaenau Ffestiniog, Sir.'

'And what did you do there, boy?'

'Saw the quarry, Sir.'

'Yes, and what did you think of it, boy?'

'Very big, Sir.'

'What was, boy?'

'The hole, Sir.'

'Anything else, boy?'

'Yes, Sir.'

'Come along then, out with it, boy.'

'Please, Sir, when are they going to fill it in?'

The boy took six of the best. For having tried to engage the master in conversation about the incontrovertible delights of Blaenau Ffestiniog, we would rifle his satchel and scribble on the pink covers of his exercise book a thesaurus of all the words we could think of for 'teacher's pet': creep, skunk, toady, rat, snitch, arse-licker, scab, blackleg, quisling, Judas ....

It will now be clear why I'm in two minds about the Old Boys' invitation: I have few rose-tinted memories to share with them. I was a bright enough lad: thanks to the teaching of Mr Don Herbert at Parc Lewis Elementary School, I had passed the entrance exam in second place among 120 boys, I worked hard at my lessons, and was not particularly unruly. True, the teachers got me through eight subjects at the Central Welsh Board exams (the equivalent of today's GCSE) but none left a lasting impression. It's only Mr Jack Reynolds, who took me for French at A Level, whom I remember with anything like respect. This martinet, a Tory snob, who had fought in the Ardennes, taught me the grammar of the language and the finer points of Romantic and Symbolist poetry that served me well when I went up to Aberystwyth in 1956 to read for a degree in French. I should be glad of the opportunity to pay him tribute, though he's been dead these many years.

But enough. I now have to decide whether I'm going to accept that invitation.

Frozen in Time

by Christine Tennent

I've got a tight hold of Lassie's lead so she won't try and bite anyone. She bites legs and feet, see. We don't know why. We think someone kicked her when she was a pup. She hates men. Except my dad.

Wendy, my sister, is sitting stiff as a pole next to me on the coach. She's too het up to speak, keeps telling me to shut up. We're going on holiday, a whole day at Mablethorpe. We've never seen the sea, not for real anyway. I've got the seat by the window. There's a woman in a grey headscarf clutching some heavy bags, all bent over and miserable. Bet she wishes she was on our coach.

Oh no: Mum's saying she's not feeling well. Surely they won't stop the coach and make us get off? I'll close my eyes. If I squeeze them tightly I won't see her pale, clammy face. Please, please don't let her faint, not again.

It's getting really stinky, what with everyone sitting squashed on top of each other and Lassie's doggy smell. I hate this silly green and red check dress: it belonged to my sister. It's too big for me. I look stupid, skinny arms and legs sticking out. My clothes are always too big or too small. Wendy's skinny like me: boys shout out sparrow legs after us. I don't care. We're on our way now; nothing's going to stop us.

I open one eye and sneak a look at Mum. Her mouth's all tight and funny looking. If she just stays still we might be all right. She's always saying she feels ill. Means she doesn't go out much. I'd feel ill if I sat in front of the fire as much as she does: it makes her legs all red and mottly. Not like Dad – he's always at the pub. Mum says he practically lives there. She won't go with him, says pubs aren't for ladies. She only has one drink a year, at Christmas. It's all yellow and slimy. 'Egg flip', Dad says it's called. He puts lemonade and a cherry in it. Mum says it makes her feel sick. I don't know why she drinks it then.

Why are we stopping already? Some of the grown-ups want to go to the lavatory. Surely they can wait a bit longer? What's wrong with them? Must be excitement.

Mum wants me to take Lassie out and let her go for a wee. 'Don't want any accidents, not on the coach.'

Mum's always worrying what other people might say. I let Lassie off the lead and she races away up the field. She's not great at coming back. I'm yelling and she's not taking any notice. I can see her in the distance.

'Lassie, come on girl!'

She's running towards me. It's like she's grinning, her pink tongue flopping out of her mouth. I can't see properly; my glasses are spattered with rain. Where's she gone?

Mum's screaming. 'Get back here now! Everyone's ready to go, we'll be left behind!'

There she is: she's somehow fallen into a ditch. She's dripping foul-smelling gloopy mud everywhere. I drag her back to the coach. Mum tries to wipe it off with some grass. She's shouting, telling me it's my fault. She raises her hand then whips it across my face.

'Ouch.' I stumble backwards as her ring catches my cheek.

'Serve you right if they don't let us back on! Silly little girl!'

Someone from the coach finds an old yellowy newspaper and we rub Lassie's coat with crumpled up paper. We make her stand on a sheet of it at the back of the coach. The Daily Express sports section, right on the racing pages, the bit Dad spends all his time looking at. Not that he ever wins anything.

An old man on the coach winks at me. 'Never mind, duck, it'll come off in the sea.'

Mum gives me a lemon sweety. It's sugary and tastes sour as well. My cheek throbs. Sometimes she uses dad's old army belt, hits us on the legs when she's really mad.

The coach is drawing into a little car park. We're here! The grown-ups are fiddling about trying to find their bags. Mum's packed us some jam sandwiches for lunch and some of her burnt currant buns. She hates cooking.

I can't breathe with that wind: it whips right up my nose, smells of salt and fish and chips.

I can hear Mum's voice: 'Do up your coats, and don't get lost!'

Me, Wendy and Lassie are running on powdery sand, crunchy with pink and purple shells. I thought the sea was blue. How come it's grey?

'Hurry up!' Wendy yells.

The wind's biting through our thin coats. What's Mum shrieking about now? We'll pretend we didn't hear. We're at the edge of the sea screaming and spinning around in the wind and rain. The waves are huge and foamy. As we run we jump over lumps of slippery green seaweed, and orangey yellow starfish staked out on the sand.

'Look at the jelly fish! You can see right through them.' They're like tiny flattened umbrellas with pinkish blobs in the middle, blowing bubbles.

'Don't get too close: they sting. Dangerous they are,' Wendy warns. She worries about everything, just like Mum.

Lassie's barking like a crazy thing, whirling round and trying to bite the waves. Wendy's plaits are flapping about: her new red ribbons have come undone. She'd better not lose them. My glasses are misted up and slipping down my nose. We're shivering and our skin's all blue-grey goose bumps.

We pull our shoes and socks off and stand in the grey sea as it tries to tug us over, sucking clammy sand between our toes. The waves are slapping our legs, tossing up spray and soaking our clothes.

There's Mum's taking a picture of Lassie with Aunty Vi's old Brownie camera.

Mum's smiling.
I'll remember this day for ever.

The Time Traveller's Disappointment
by Jennie Tripp

The five hour time difference meant that one of us had to stay up late or get up early, and for that year and a half, I woke faithfully at five thirty, found my socks in the dark and edged downstairs, leaving the computer to boot up while I boiled the kettle. I always glanced at the BBC Scotland homepage before opening the game interface, entering my password and taking my first sip of steaming coffee.

Eddie was usually there before me, getting tired, raiding the breadbin and watching his friends log out one by one until my username turned green to show I was online. On screen, we were dressed in heavy armour and weapons that boasted of our high skill levels, while in reality, we were both in our pyjamas.

It was just before Christmas when we first met, chopping trees in the virtual forest. That day, it was me who stayed up late, while he was watching the Massachusetts snow from his window and looking forward to dinner. He told me that he was a mixed-up American with Hungarian grandparents; I confessed to being a budding scientist and added him to my list of online friends.

We soon fell into a routine, and he began to spill over into my everyday life, as I did into his. During lectures, I would replay our conversations and we both looked forward to sharing the everyday bits and bobs of our lives. Some nights, I would fall asleep at the keyboard and some mornings, he would stay awake until I left for college. We spent endless hours together, divided by an ocean, while other players began to feel uncomfortable around us.

'Get a room!' we'd hear, sometimes in capitals, to show they were really yelling, and more and more, we desperately wanted to do just that. Sharing a fantasy of opening our own breakfast café in Amsterdam, we agreed on background jazz, argued over the decor and carefully unravelled our linguistic differences.

Our sleepy logouts became painful and prolonged as we found ourselves head over heels in love.

Then, one lunchtime, I logged on and he was already there, just out of bed.

'I've picked up a passport form,' he announced, 'and dropped out of school.'

I knew that he was very tall and would be carrying a backpack and guitar, but as I sat nervously on the metal bench at Edinburgh bus station, I still worried that I might not recognise him. After all, he wouldn't be brandishing a poisoned dagger, or at least, I hoped not. On the other hand, he was about to discover that I didn't really have pigtails, or jewellery that could teleport us out of trouble. Then suddenly he was in front of me, in his oversized coat, and after eighteen months of longing, we finally hugged, with my head tucked under his chin and his fingers interlocked in the small of my back.

Back at my house, I made coffee. I already knew he liked his white, without sugar, but as we gripped our hot drinks, I found myself gazing, not at my swashbuckling lover, but at a sandy-haired American stranger. Eddie seemed embarrassed and tongue-tied, and recoiled when I moved to put my hand on his. I wasn't ready for this. In our unreal world, he had been unfailingly tender but now, on my sofa, his dismay at discovering that I paid little resemblance to that skinny avatar in red boots was palpable.

He unpacked his misshapen t-shirts, bundled them into the washing machine and ran a bath. We'd once laughed together at the idea of his elongated frame getting comfortable in a tub designed for someone much shorter. I'd pictured his feet dangling over the edge, one either side of the taps, but now, the thought of him naked unsettled me. Despite months of imagining myself enveloped in his giant arms, it went without saying that he would sleep in the spare room.

Next morning, rejuvenated by the May sunshine and hidden

behind sunglasses, I took Eddie on a city tour, pausing to photograph old buildings and interesting trees, hoping to revive the spark we'd ignited in our virtual world. I asked plenty of questions, but already knew the answers to most of them, and when we turned the corner to the sandwich shop I'd described, I knew exactly what he would order. After we'd eaten, we lay down side by side on the grass.

'I was thinking of moving on tomorrow.'

His footsteps were already receding with every breath.

'I'm going to take the train to London.'

I rustled up the perfect full Scottish: two fried eggs with glistening yolks and crisp edges, pork sausages, a grilled tomato, Heinz beans, mushrooms, plus a potato scone, knowing it was as close as we'd ever get to Amsterdam. As I loaded the dishwasher, I watched him pack the last of his boxers and notebooks, wondering what he had written about me, almost unable to bear the idea of his disappointment being recorded for posterity.

Finally, at the station, he double checked that he had his camera and tickets, and then he was gone.

'Have a safe journey!' I shouted after him. It seemed the right thing to say.

The imprint of his half-hearted goodbye hug stayed on my skin for days, but after a decent interval, I began getting up at five thirty again and waiting for him by the trees. I knew we had crossed a line that could never be redrawn, but hoped we could salvage a friendship from the ruins. Many players wandered past me, offered random greetings and moved on, but Eddie never came my way again. My gentle time-traveller had slipped back into the middle of the night, but every morning for months, as I poured my coffee, I imagined him half asleep across the sea, toasting the last piece of potato bread and planning his next great adventure.

The Red Velvet Jacket
by Jayne Walter

'When's Mam coming home, Nan?' I asked, in between mouthfuls of egg, beans and chips. Nan made brilliant chips.

'I don't know, love. Later. Eat your food.'

'Where's Dad taken her?'

'Into town.'

'Is he taking us home?'

'Eat your tea.'

'I need the toilet.'

'Go on then. You know where it is ….'

I got up, shuffled through the tiny kitchen, out of the back door and past the tin bath that was hanging on the outside wall. The wooden door squeaked open, as I leaned over the wooden toilet seat to check for spiders. I always had to check for spiders, because they could bite you while you had a wee. There were none there today, but still I had to check.

It was cold in there; the draft came under the door and froze my bum as I crouched in mid-air over the seat. I gazed around at the dark corners. I couldn't imagine anything managing to live in weather as cold as this. But I had to check.

'Did you remember to wash your hands?'

'Yes.' But I hadn't. I couldn't get the water thing to work without burning my hands. Nan said it was called a geezer, and I thought that was a strange name for a water thingie. A geezer was something I heard Minder talking about on the telly, and not a tap.

We didn't use the geezer to fill the tin bath, either. On Sunday nights, Nan would fill four massive saucepans with water and put them on top of the cooker, so that I could get in the bath and wash myself, with the inch or so of water just covering my skinny little legs. Had to be clean for school on a Monday.

'I don't want any more food, Nan.'

'You've hardly touched it. Just eat a couple of beans, then.'

'Shall I pack my bag, Nan ... if we're going home with Dad?' I'd already packed it, and left it under Nan's old feather bed, the one that two of her husbands had died in.

'No.'

'When's Mam coming home?'

'Later.'

'But how long will she be?'

'Here we are, go and sit on the settee, watch some telly,' she said, sighing, and putting the Redifusion black and white TV on.

It was Saturday night. *Crackerjack*. I liked *Crackerjack*. I sat on the corduroy settee, and watched kids running around, playing games and keeping scores. There was lots of cheering, lots of noise. Nan sat at the table, staring into space, rocking gently from side to side like she did when she was thinking.

In they piled, my mother with a face like thunder, and my father, likewise. They both stank of whisky. My mother was wearing a red velvet jacket, which she hadn't been wearing when she went out earlier.

'What's the matter with you, woman?' my father yelled at my mother.

'You'll never bloody change, Ken.'

'Are we going home?' I asked my mother. Silence.

Nan walked out into the kitchen and put the whistler kettle on the cooker. Tea. She drank lots of tea. I hated tea when I was ten.

'Nothing's ever good enough for you. Took you for a steak dinner, bought you that jacket ... still you've got a face like a smacked arse.'

My brother had told my mother that him and my dad were living on bone stew last week, and the landlord had said they had to leave because the rent hadn't been paid again. Nan had posted ten pounds to them in Porthcawl for food. Dad must have strayed out of the pub and got some work, my nan said when he turned up earlier, flashing the notes.

'You think that's going to make it alright do you? A bit of grub, a couple of drinks and this bloody thing?' She tore the sleeve as she pulled the jacket off, and I ducked as it landed on the back of the settee.

'I just don't understand you, woman. You're calling time on twenty-five years of marriage. Do you want to end up like your mother, with ten different dicks inside you?'

I looked at my mother. Her face was getting pinker. I looked at my father. His cheeks were red. They matched his eyes. I knew what a dick was, because Linda, my brother's girlfriend, had given me the talk a couple of months before. On a wet Tuesday afternoon, when I was off school with a stomach ache.

'You BASTARD!' My nan flew through the kitchen door, and landed a prime right hook up against my father's chin. His six-foot frame stumbled backwards, into the under stairs cupboard door – the same cupboard where Nan kept her late brother's plastic arm, from the war. My father's eyes were glazed with the shock of getting a clout from his five-foot-two mother-in-law.

'Oh, you've really blown it now, pal,' screamed my mother as she stepped in between the two of them.

My father said nothing.

And I tried to look around three pairs of legs to see what Stupot was doing now. And I knew that I wasn't going home. Not today.

Do-Re-Mi-Oh-No

by Lauren Williamson

I remember so vividly the most public humiliation I ever encountered. I was seven years old and my teacher had just announced to the class that the school was holding a talent contest. I held the title of Teacher's Pet and knew that I needed to uphold it. I just had to find the perfect talent.

My mum and sister teased me about my singing, so I knew that wouldn't be an option. And as for dancing, we never afforded dance lessons, so back then I never knew I had rhythm. Besides, all the posh girls in the class would be doing a little ballet performance or extracting a famous song from a musical that I'd never heard of, let alone seen.

But one thing I could do was play 'Do-Re-Mi' on the piano. Proudly I informed Miss Wood and she was every bit as impressed as I wanted her to be.

We'd only one week to prepare for the contest which was being held in the main hall. The schoolchildren would be the audience with three teachers judging. As the days counted down and the tension mounted, I could sense there was great excitement around my piano playing. My friends were amazed. My mother was even more amazed.

'I never knew you had lessons,' said one.

'You? Play the piano?' asked another.

'But you don't even have a telephone: how come you can play the piano?'

I told my friends that my dad owned a piano and taught me. This was not as grand as it sounded, honestly. He owned an electric keyboard and it was one of his step-daughters who taught me on a seasonal visit to them. And besides, it was only the first bit of the song that I could play.

On the morning of the contest, I was very impressed with myself. I felt very proud and grown up, like a ten-year-old. Me, Lauren Townsend, playing the piano in a contest!

Me, Lauren Townsend playing the piano … OH MY GOD! What am I doing?

Slamming headfirst into my senses I knew there was only one thing to do. Tell my teacher. She liked me. She would understand.

Morning came to an abrupt halt and we were ushered to the hall. I needed to bail out now. There was no way I could go through with this. I had been so silly and let all this self-enthusiasm carry me on a tide towards the cliff.

'Miss Wood, I don't want to do the contest,' I said meekly, holding out for offers of special treatment.

'Why, what's wrong?' She mothered me. I was scared of letting her down. I adored my teacher and craved her approval on everything from my times tables to my plaits.

'I … can't really play the piano,' I said sincerely.

'Don't be silly! Of course you can. You wouldn't enter if you couldn't play.'

'But, I can't,' I gasped, holding onto hope.

'It'll all be over soon and you will be glad you did it then. Run along and good luck.' She smiled, shooing me backstage.

All the children sat cross-legged facing the stage, witnessing surprise performances from some of the boys who did a play and one girl who played the clarinet. We were spectators to some truly boring dancing from three girls who clearly thought they bagged it. As each talent went before the judges I felt more scared. And stupid. It was only a matter of time before it was my turn. An older girl was now up to play the piano.

'You can read music!' commented an impressed judge looking at her music book.

That did it. I was a nervous wreck knowing too well I was about to face ultimate humiliation.

'Lauren Townsend?' called a judge.

My legs moved and the rest followed, with by brain trailing far behind. Heavily I made my way and sat at the piano. I sang along in my head as I played each note: Doe, a deer, a female deer, Ray, a drop of golden suuuuuun …. That was all I knew. It was far too short. I hesitated as I realised more was expected from me, so like a true professional, the show went on. I played and played.

I'm not sure how long it went on for, but I'd hazard a guess at four minutes. I thought my supplement of exclusive, never heard before music wasn't bad at all. I felt a hint of optimism as I focused on the black and white keys, willing them to be harmonious. Then I went back to my familiar fourteen notes, followed by another four minutes of unsystematically pushing down piano keys. I decided that should be enough to get me somewhere ahead of last place and finished with a grand finale of my now legendary fourteen notes.

There was no round of applause like there was for all the other acts, including for the girl who sang 'Baa Baa Black Sheep'. I clearly had one friend there as she clapped for me. And that was it. Even the judges were stunned into silence. I turned around to face my audience, The Schoolchildren. The stillness in a hall with so many people was unsettling. They were actually embarrassed for me. They even had the decency to hold back any heckling or spitting chewed-up paper bullets through an inkless biro.

As I sat back in my seat, I felt the eyes boring into me would be there for many terms. Shame really as I turned out to be a very good dancer and dance coach!

But to my relief I was let off the hook of all mockery as it turns out there was a more memorable performance than my own perfectly disastrous one: Mickey Spittal poo'd his pants.

Wednesday's Child

by Georgina Wilson

It's always a Wednesday, so I'm sure of the day when we let ourselves in. Auntie Hazel, who isn't really my auntie, but my godmother, is a fat woman, squashed into a tiny room at the back of a house. She always sits in an armchair near a gas fire with brown mottles on her legs.

'Say hello to Auntie Hazel,' Mam says, sinking into a chair further away from the fire because she doesn't want mottles. I shuffle myself onto a leather stool, from where I see piles of books, like colourful towers, shooting up behind chairs and in corners. As usual I long to touch them but I can't read yet and Auntie will glare at me through piggy round eyes if I so much as move.

'He said this, she said that, bla and bla,' they drone on, a round of sameness, that I never properly listen to. Instead I rock back and forth on the stool; in time to the tick ticking of a huge wooden clock, which Auntie calls the old gentleman.

Walled shelves, where books might have been, are instead cluttered with ugly faced jugs. Next to the old gentleman is a glass fronted cabinet. Through the glass I take in each colourful part of the kings and queens and different china dogs.

'What's that one called?' I ask Auntie.

'Shush, we're talking,' she says flicking me away with her hand.

'It's as well I never had kid's cos I might ave 'armed em.' Armed, I suppose means been tightly squeezed in her vast flabby arms until you're completely flat.

As we leave we bump into Uncle Bill. He has a red clown face and wears a dusty boiler suit.

'Hello.' He crouches down. 'What's your name?'

'Georgina.'

'That's a mouthful.' He fetches me a three-penny bit from a jar in the pantry.

All the way home, on the back of Mam's bike, I turn the coin over and over in my duffle coat pocket, tracing with my finger and thumb each straight edge and the raised part with the buttercup flower. In front of me there is Mam, dark hair beneath a see-through headscarf, spindly legs pushing the pedals round and round, her striped skirt blowing out in the wind.

'Hold on tight,' she says.

'What's a Godmother?' I ask.

'Someone that cares for you if your Mam dies,' she says and the bike wobbles.

When I start school the sun has disappeared and we've to battle against the wind. Mam holds my hand. Leaves whip up into my face and there's a heavy feeling in my tummy. The school building is new. Builders help us across planks of wood covering a trench. They are sorry. It should have been concreted over and gates up but there's been delays.

At first I don't realise Mam's gone. My eyes are busy darting around. In one corner of the classroom there is a Wendy house with red and white check curtains. Inside are miniature pots and pans and a pretend sink and cooker. Miss Taylor wears a green dress that's the shape of a barrel. When she tells us to sit on low chairs around a table, her face puckers around her eyes and at the edges of her mouth, which makes me think she's kind.

But the other children have odd faces, like misshapen gremlins or nasty dwarfs. Some are pale, some rosy, some have black hair, others ginger or blonde. A fat girl sucks the ends of her hair. A boy fiddles with his tie on elastic. I haven't seen many children before and I don't like these or want to be with them.

Weeks later, Mam's in her chair and I notice her tummy is

fatter.

'Could you go to the shop for a quarter of salted peanuts?' she says. From then on that's all she does, sit in a chair eating salted peanuts. I'm sad because I remember when we used to go out together on the bike.

One Wednesday I push open the door and call out, 'It's me, I'm home.' I've a painting of a bright yellow duck that I can't wait to show her. But her chair by the fire is empty. Aunty Hazel is standing by the French doors. Her podgy face goes into a lopsided smile when she sees me. She says Mam is in hospital and I've not to worry. She calls me pet and makes me chips and egg, which I can't eat. When Dad comes home I ask, 'What does dying mean?'

A few days later I'm allowed to stay off school because Mam is coming home with a surprise. I think it might be a bike with stabilisers. When I hear the squeak of the front door I run towards it.

Mam looks different. There is a white bundle in her arms. I back off when I see it.

'This is David,' she says, 'Your new baby brother. Would you like to hold him?'

I definitely don't want to. His head looks big. He's like the crying boy in a picture that every house has on the wall.

'Where's it from? Take it back,' I scream. Dad sits me on his knee, strokes my hair and I snuggle into his chest smelling the familiar malty beer on his breath. I don't need a brother and soon I know it will be him going out on the bike with Mam on Wednesdays instead of me.

Author Biographies

Jo Austen

Jo Austen is forty-something and completed her MA in Creative Writing (Christchurch Canterbury) last year. She taught art for twelve years before taking a sharp turn at the traffic lights and now runs an industrial abseiling company. She hopes that one day her small-holding and writing will enable her to give up the day job.

Trina Beckett

Trina lives in Cornwall and recently rediscovered a passion for writing. She has had articles published in miniatures magazines, travel magazines and *Cornwall Today*. Her short stories have been highly commended, and her most recent included in the shortlist for the Brit Writers' Awards, (the winner yet to be announced!). She works as a one-to-one tutor in schools and higher education, and is currently completing a Writers Bureau course. In her spare time, Trina enjoys coastal walking and playing the drums. She has been happily married for thirty-five years to military historian Ian, and has two grown up children and three adorable grandchildren.

Suzanne Bellenger

Suzanne Bellenger is struggling with the notion that one should concentrate on one genre of writing, and has written plays, short stories, children's stories and even characterisations for hotel themes. The only thing she generally avoids is pottering in poetry, as it's mostly Jackson Pollock to her. She is now trying to discipline herself to focus on one area and is writing her first novel.

Pascale Bientot

Pascale Bientot is studying creative writing at Newcastle University.

P. de Burlet

P. de Burlet found an old photo of her four-year old self, her eight-year old sister and her father; all of them were naked, on a beach. The photo, taken in the 1950s, represents a contradiction. Her very proper father, RAF and later FO, was a naturist. Without his uniform he was a kind and funny person. Her career highlights include train cleaner, zookeeper (insects & small mammals), artist and art teacher. She currently has a 'proper job' in arts education (paid holidays) and she makes things. She began to write stories a while back and is now working on a second novel; the first is consigned to the great Word doc. in the basement.

Tracy Burton

Tracy Burton is a frustrated local government communication officer living near Newport. Tracy juggles her writing around family commitments (partner, three daughters, two granddaughters) and a passion for long-distance hiking and travel. Minor successes spur her on, e.g. she was shortlisted in the BBC Wales It's My Shout 2009 competition, and she's currently working on a feature-length script. Tracy's perfect life would see the day job disappear completely and lots of writing, hiking and travel take its place; her sister says she's a dreamer....

Dolly Carter

Dolly Carter came to England in the early 1950s and separated from her husband soon after her first daughter was born. She worked as a dentist in London where she met her second husband to whom she was happily married for forty-three years until his death. She enjoys trying out new activities, including water-colour painting. She recently took a beginners' course in playing the harp at Edinburgh Harp Festival, along with her daughter and granddaughter – the harpist in the family! This memoir is her first attempt at writing and is in memory of her lovely mother who died when she was nine years of age. She will be eighty in December.

Jane Common

Jane Common is a freelance journalist living in south-east London with her Battersea dog Attlee and her formerly stray cat Dodger. Since taking a course in creative writing five years ago she has been pottering around penning the occasional short story but her inclusion in the Leaf Books Memoir Anthology, the first time she has ever had any of her literary efforts published, will, hopefully, spur her on to write more.

Wendy Craig

Wendy Craig has been a teacher, freelance writer specialising in articles on travel and history, and small business owner. Recently she returned to writing, concentrating mainly on short stories. Several of these have been published in newspapers and magazines and broadcast on national radio. Born in New Zealand, Wendy has also lived in England and Greece. She combines her love of travel with her hobbies of taking photographs and people watching. She now lives with her husband in a small country town in New Zealand, taking much inspiration from the natural beauty of the surrounding area.

Jane Croft

Jane Croft has been a full-time writer and novelist since 2004. Thus far she has four historical romances to her credit. These are published by Harlequin and appear under her pseudonym, Joanna Fulford. She has written numerous articles that have appeared in magazines both here and overseas and, more recently, has begun to achieve a measure of success with short stories. She writes poetry for the love of it, and her work has appeared in various publications including the *Thomas Hardy Society Journal* and *Agenda*.

Ian Cundell

Ian Cundell is a freelance hack (sometimes), a PR advisor (sometimes), a web designer (sometimes) and a business analyst (you will have detected a theme here). His school report said he was 'relaxed to the point of coma', which is odd given how grumpy he is. When not being a grumpy, but relaxed, portfolio career holder he is chairman of Verulam Writers' Circle in St Albans, where he wields his hammer with equal opportunities grumpiness. Not unreasonably he thinks VWC is the best writers' group around.

Frank Ferrie

Frank Ferrie is a writer and painter. He teaches art and art history in various locations in London and Sussex. Frank has never studied writing formally, but has been mulling over short stories for a number of years. In 2007 he was shortlisted for BBC radio 4's Opening Lines. He is currently writing his first novel, *Down and Out in Hampton Court*. Frank lives with his wife in a small terraced house in Worthing, West Sussex. He writes in the upper back bedroom whilst his wife watches television and eats chocolate.

Lesley Fuller

Lesley Fuller lives in Kent. She has recently retired from teaching Adult Literacy, giving her more time to devote to her love of words, a passion since childhood. She has joined her local writers' group and is looking forward to continuing to enjoy the writers she is meeting and working with. She has had two poems published previously, reading them aloud at the anthology launch night. Lesley is currently working on performance poetry and planning her debut locally this summer (the writers' group says!!).

Sue Gill

Sue Gill lives in a wooden beach house above the shoreline in Cumbria, with her artist husband and close to their three grandchildren. Her career peaked early. At twenty-three she was a headteacher in the wilds of North Yorkshire, then gave it up to be a street theatre performer, truck driver, cook and nomadic celebratory artist. Author of the *Dead Good Funerals Book* and other *Dead Good Guides* to rites of passage, she currently works as an independent celebrant, creating secular ceremonies which mark birth, death and many occasions in between.

David Grubb

David Grubb has published widely. *Fire Child* was published by Leaf in 2010 and his latest poetry collection is due from Shearsman in 2011, and also a collection of short stories.

Tamara Guhrs

Tamara Guhrs lives in a bustling African city but carries calming memories of the vast, elephant-populated wilderness she grew up in. Tamara is a playwright, deeply committed to using theatre as an activism tool to understand issues of poverty and environment in southern Africa. She teaches drama at Wits University. She has written a book on Zambian traditional ceremonies and rituals, and is quietly gathering the courage to publish some of her fiction.

Ursula Hurley

Ursula Hurley divides her time between Ormskirk, where she gardens, and Salford, where she works. Inspired by the natural world, she writes poetry and prose, with a particular interest in creative non-fiction. She has just published her first poetry chapbook, *Tree* (Erbacce Press, 2009), and is currently seeking a publisher for her experimental memoir, *Heartwood*.

Paul Jenkins

Paul Jenkins has just completed a Creative Writing degree at the University of Glamorgan. He is obsessed with writing short stories, telling tall stories and watching his weight move in the opposite direction to his bank balance. When not making outlandish status updates on Facebook, he can be found in drunken repose in Penarth.

Freda Love Smith

Freda Love Smith is an American drummer, songwriter and fiction writer. She has published several short stories with Leaf, including 'Jesse and Jesus,' which won first prize in Leaf's 2008 Micro-fiction competition, and has also been published in *The Yellow Room* magazine, *The Nottingham Trent University Creative Writing Anthology* and *Critical Studies*. She is currently completing a Master's degree in Creative Writing and is working on a novel.

Liz Martinez

Liz Martinez was a medical negligence lawyer for many years before leaving the legal profession in 2003 to raise a family. She began writing children's books in 2006. Her first children's book *Angel Seeds* was published in 2008. *The Everyday Witch* was published by Bloomsbury in October 2009. Lately she has started writing short stories and flash fiction for adults, and may even finish her novel one day. Liz also has a strong interest in spiritual studies, spiritual development and spiritual healing. She lives in Berkshire with her two children.

Alison McNaught

Alison McNaught, 52, is a freelance bid-writer, making funding applications for the charitable sector. She has been writing creatively, on and off, for ten years. In 2006 she completed a part-time Certificate in Creative Writing at the University of Kent. Since 2007 she has been studying for a BA Hons Degree in English Literature with the Open University. She has recently had poetry published in Australia and Britain. 'Crows in the Toilet' was written in response to an exercise that asked the writer to describe her first experience of fear. Alison's ambition is to go on to study for an MA in Creative Writing and to complete her novel.

Moira McPartlin

Moira McPartlin is a Scot with Irish roots. Although born in the Scottish Borders, she was brought up in a Fife mining village. She has had work published in *Storie, People's Friend, Countryside Tales, The Stirling Observer* and T*he Scottish Mountaineer* and regularly contributes book reviews and articles to www.laurahird.com. Recent awards in the Bournemouth Short Story Competition and the Scottish Association of Writers Novel Competition help to sustain Moira's determination to succeed. She is currently seeking a publisher for her novel, *The Incomers*.

Moira is one of the organizers for Weegie Wednesday, a monthly book industry networking event held in Glasgow and sits on the editorial board of New Voices Press, the publishing arm of the Federation of Writers (Scotland).

She lives in Stirlingshire with her husband.

Diana Mitchener

Diana Mitchener took an M.A. in Creative Writing at University College Chichester in 2000 after retiring as a senior lecturer. She is actively involved in writing groups in West Sussex and enjoys performing her work. Short stories and poems have been placed in several competitions and published in anthologies: *Sussex Seams, Biscuit, Cannon's Mouth, Cruse Poetry, Roundyhouse* and *French Literary Review*. *Ten Poems for Performance* and a collection of poetry entitled *Corncockle* were published in 2009 (www.corncockle.co.uk). Now in her seventies Diana is examining the effect of childhood experiences on her adult life.

Eithne Nightingale

Besides working as Head of Diversity at the V&A, Eithne Nightingale writes travel, fiction and memoir for publication in the UK and Australia. Recent successes include winning two categories of the Arts Council sponsored Writers.Inc Award in 2008 for a children's story inspired by the story of a Rwandan refugee and for a travel article, 'The Back Streets of Beijing'. She has read out part of her memoir, based on life in a northern vicarage in the 1950s, on Lancashire radio. She is also a photographer. For more details of awards, publications and photography see www.eithnenightingale.com.

Amy O'Neil

Amy loves sitting in cafés reading for hours, and she thinks that writing short stories is one of the greatest treats in life! She also draws, paints, dances and eats excessive amounts of chocolate. Since graduating from Art school three years ago, she has found writing fiction to be a more fitting way of expressing herself and making her ideas visible. She is still very much learning the craft, but so far her short stories have won places in several small competitions, as well as being recently shortlisted for the Fish Short Story Prize.

Clarissa Pattern

Clarissa Pattern imagines a world full of unicorns and a time when she earns enough money from writing to justify to her husband all the hours she spends tapping away at the keyboard. Currently the unicorns are the most realistic dream. In between living her more interesting fantasy life she worries about her children, walks the dog, cooks occasionally edible meals and exorcises all the bad things that have happened to her through her stories.

Karen Phillips

Karen currently lives in Edinburgh and has happily committed to staying there for at least another year. She always carries notebook and pen with her just in case – you never know when words come. This is her first published story, although there are many just lurking about in tatty notebooks and on the C drive of a dodgy laptop.

Clare Potter

Clare Potter is a performance poet/writer brought up in Blackwood, South Wales. She graduated from the University of Southern Mississippi with an MA in Afro–Caribbean literature. She then moved to New Orleans, where she was a consultant for the New Orleans Writing Project. On returning to Wales after ten years, Clare won the 2004 John Tripp Award for Spoken Poetry and her collection *spilling histories* was published (Cinnamon, 2006). In the last few years, Clare has been involved in collaborative projects with other writers, musicians and artists.

Brenda Ray

Brenda Ray has worked at various times in librarianship and as a creative writing tutor. She worked for some years as a freelance playwright and now concentrates mainly on the short story form. Her collection of stories, *The Siren of Salamanca*, was published by Leaf Books in 2008. She has a degree in Photographic Studies from the University of Derby, where she based her dissertation on history seen through the eyes of family photographs, which often serve as an inspiration for her short stories.

Joyce Reed

Joyce Reed is a retired music teacher and writer with several self-published collections of short stories and poems. Her self-published book *Teachers Monday Flowers,* which contains poems illustrated by her original water colour paintings, sold out on the day of publication. Her poems appear regularly in anthologies, and she has won many Writers news/Writing magazine competitions, and has been Poet of the year, and Winner of winners in the David St John Thomas charitable trust competitions. Principal poetic influences are the natural world and our place within it. Recently she set up the successful

Marple writing competition, which this year is for Poetry. When not writing she enjoys gardening, walking in the Derbyshire and Cheshire countryside, and reading psychological thrillers.

Claire Riviere

Claire Riviere lives in North Norfolk. She works for two antiquarian booksellers as a cataloguer, which keeps her extremely busy. When she is not working she tries to make time for writing. She has completed several courses in Norwich and has recently enrolled on a course at the University of East Anglia. Her aim is to produce a collection of short stories.

Nick Robinson

Nick Robinson has been writing newspaper and magazine articles since 1978, and fiction since 2001. Having completed a series of creative writing courses at Lancaster University, Nick began an MA in Creative Writing at Manchester Metropolitan University in 2003, and graduated in 2007. Among his favourite contemporary authors are Nick Hornby, John O'Farrell and Sebastian Faulks, while his top ten novels include works such as David Mitchell's *Cloud Atlas* and Chimamanda Adichie's *Purple Hibiscus*. Nick has written numerous short stories, co-authored a play that was performed in Lancaster, and is currently looking for a publisher for his debut novel, *Starchasers*.

Sylvia Sanderson

Sylvia Sanderson, married with three grown up children, is a musician/teacher and lives in Hertfordshire. In 1995 she became Area Music Principal for Hertfordshire Music Service. She has written for the educational press and has had various short stories and articles published. Her poems have appeared in *Poetry Now, A Woman's Place, First Time, The Darius Poetry anthology, The Peoples' Poet* and *Parameter magazine*. In 1998 Piper Ash published an anthology of her poems: *Signals in the Dark*. In 2008 she won Emissary Publishing Comic Novel competition and her novel *Changing Places* was published in 2009.

David Craig Smith

David Craig Smith was born in Manchester in 1936, long enough ago to have forgotten the discomfort of cold, pre-central heating bedrooms and the tedium of days confined to bed with childhood illnesses. He now looks fondly back on those days with a carefully selective memory. He began writing when he retired from work some twelve years ago, has had one play produced locally and short stories published in a variety of magazines and anthologies and on internet sites. He lives in Berkshire and is a member of Slough Writers group.

Meic Stephens

Meic Stephens was born in Trefforest in 1938. He was educated at the UCW, Aberystwyth, the UCNW, Bangor, and the University of Rennes. He taught French at Ebbw Vale before joining the staff of the *Western Mail* in Cardiff and, from 1967 to 1990, was Literature Director of the Welsh Arts Council.

Until his retirement in 2003 he was Professor of Welsh Writing in English at the University of Glamorgan, where he taught Journalism. He founded *Poetry Wales* in 1965 and edited the magazine for eight years. He has edited, translated and written about 160 books, including *The Companion to the Literature of Wales*. He contributes obituaries of eminent Welsh people to *The Independent* and writes poetry in Welsh, his second language.

Christine Tennent

Christine Tennent was born in Derby and now lives in Buckinghamshire with her family, which includes a large Red Setter and a tiny Puggle. Christine has written mainly short stories and poetry since she was young and has an English and History degree from Leeds University. Since taking an early retirement from the Open University's Human Resources department she has been able to concentrate on writing and has had several poems published. She has also just given birth to two children's stories that are now seeking a home.

Jennie Tripp

Jennie has dabbled in science, singing and sandwich-making but is never happier than when perched on her favourite chair with her laptop and a tumbler of Sauvignon Blanc, checking out the latest showbiz gossip whilst waiting for a flash of literary inspiration. Jennie enjoys writing in many different styles, but her impatience often steers her towards micro-fiction and short poems, both of which have a bad habit of popping into her head at unbelievably awkward moments.

Jayne Walter

Jayne Walter is a Graduate of the University of Glamorgan's Creative Writing degree programme. In her former life she has been a Holiday Rep, a Sales Manager and a Reflexologist. She is studying for an M.A in Creative Writing at the University of Wales, Swansea. She hopes to – eventually – earn enough to buy a Tuscan Villa, where she will hibernate for months on end and just write ….

Lauren Williamson

Lauren lives in Kent with her husband and two young children. She has been enjoying flirtatious liaisons with writing since June 2009 as she was made redundant and, being a working parent, never had the time before then. Her recent encounters include a short story idea for magazines and a children's story inspired by stories by Julia Donaldson (*The Gruffalo*). This is the first piece of work she has had published and the success has encouraged her to continue to develop her writing ability.

Georgina Wilson

Georgina Wilson is a mature student studying Creative Writing at The University of Hull. She has recently had a ten minute monologue called *The Blue Umbrella* showcased in a 'find your voice' event at The Hull Truck Theatre. Her hobbies are dog walking, antique hunting and reading. At present she is working on a memoir called *The Slave's Dream* and a crime novel called *Flames of the night*.